Amitabh Pandey studied Economics at St Stephen's College and the Delhi School of Economics, Delhi University. He has taught at an undergraduate college of Delhi University, worked for many years for the Government of India, and built software systems in the private sector.

Amitabh finally retired to Noida to read and perchance to write.

HIMALAYAN REFUGE

Amitabh Pandey

SPEAKING
TIGER

SPEAKING TIGER BOOKS LLP
125A, Ground Floor, Shahpur Jat, near Asiad Village,
New Delhi 110049

First published by Speaking Tiger Books in 2024

ISBN: 978-93-5447-796-6
eISBN: 978-93-5447-855-0

10 9 8 7 6 5 4 3 2 1

Typeset in Baskerville MT Std by SÜRYA, New Delhi
Printed at HT Media Ltd, Greater Noida

This one is for my uncle, Subodh Kumar Pande, with gratitude for reaffirming the value of books and permitting unrestricted access to his private library for as long as I can remember.

1

Dana parked her motorbike in front of Singh Sweets in the Haldwani Bazaar and entered the restaurant with a duffel bag in one hand and a backpack on her shoulders. She was hot and tired after a long and frustrating ride from Delhi on a blazing summer morning. A traffic jam at Garhmukteshwar had ruined her plan to be in the mountains by nine o'clock.

Singh Sahib's youngest daughter-in-law, who was manning the till, welcomed Dana warmly and led her to a corner table.

'So wonderful to see you,' gushed Gurpreet as she summoned a waiter to take Dana's order. 'Terribly hot, isn't it, and it's only ten o'clock! When did you start from Delhi? Did you meet a lot of traffic at Garh? There's a big Ganga snan today and that always jams up traffic on the bridge.'

Dana smiled and nodded. It was difficult to get in a word edge-ways when Gurpreet was in full flow.

Cold water was served, the food order taken, Gurpreet returned to her post, and Dana leaned back in her chair and surveyed the room carefully.

The restaurant was, as always, doing roaring business. Knowledgeable tourists driving up to the hills, others driving down on their way home, all stopped at Singh Sweets for the superb, reasonably priced food, the clean loos and efficient service. At a corner table, however, Dana noted three rough-looking young men who were definitely not tourists on holiday.

'Very nice, very nice indeed,' observed one of the toughs, aka Chintu Tiwari, eying Dana boldly.

'Hmmm, yes. Solid maal: juicy, and foreign, I think,' replied Ashok, the alpha male of the group—the tallest, strongest and most brutal.

Billu, the youngest, simply nodded.

'Let's take her, if she's going up to the mountains,' suggested Chintu.

'You're fucking horny this morning! Didn't get enough last night at Champa's?'

'What to do, boss, I am like that only. So, what do you say, Ashok Bhai, lets pick her up, eh, and party at our old place—haven't been there in a long time.'

Ashok thought for a while. 'Ok, motherfuckers, let's do it—but no rough stuff in public. Boss doesn't like it. I'll offer her some good quality dope—once these bitches smoke a couple of joints, they're ready to fuck a regiment! Finish eating and go get the gaadi. I'll follow her out when she leaves and chat her up. Wait for my signal.'

'But…' Chintu began to protest and Ashok turned on him with a snarl.

'You do as you are told, you miserable bastard! You'll get your share don't worry. Now get a fucking move on!'

Chintu and young Billu left quickly. Nobody argued with Ashok in a bad mood—and his mood swings were always violent and unpredictable.

Dana noted the long appraising looks directed towards her—predator evaluating prey—and something dark and violent welled up inside her, involuntary and overwhelming. She took a deep breath.

'Easy girl, you are on holiday. Just let it be and let them be too. Unless, of course, they come asking for it.'

She had a leisurely meal, then used the washroom and sat for a while relishing the calm. The bill paid, she picked up her bags, waved Gurpreet goodbye and strolled out into the heat.

He came up to her as she finished securing her luggage to the pillion.

'Hi there, good morning,' he said, starting his confident man-about-town routine. 'I'm Ashok.'

Dana gave him a friendly smile and a pleasant, 'Hi, I'm Dana.'

'Nice bike! A bit rough for a pretty lady, I would have thought,' remarked Ashok.

'I like 'em rough and I can handle them, no worries,' replied Dana.

'Great! Going up to the hills?' asked Ashok.

'Yes—too darned hot in the plains now. I'm going to drive all over the Himalayas for a month!'

'Lucky you. I have a living to make or I'd come along!'

'Some company would have been nice! Are you from around here?'

'Yes. Anything I can help you with?'

Dana hesitated, and then took a decision. She looked around carefully, as any tourist looking to score a little dope would, and smiled. 'Actually, I was told you could get some good stuff, you know, around here. Something for a little happiness on a lonely evening.'

Ashok smiled back. 'If I'm guessing right about your needs, then I have just the stuff for you—top quality guaranteed. In fact, my friends and I were planning to drive up to a lovely picnic spot up there,' he gestured towards the looming mountains, 'and party a little. Care to join us?'

Dana looked thoughtful for a moment, then said, 'Sure, just for a while though, and then I have to be on my way. And no funny business, ok? I can look after myself, just so you know.'

Ashok grinned broadly. 'Oh, we're not that sort, Dana—worry not. There are the boys; come, put your bags in the vehicle and I'll ride with you to show you the way.'

'That's a pain—I've just tied up all my stuff. Why don't you lead and I'll follow.'

Ashok reluctantly agreed and led the way out of town and up the mountain towards Bhimtal.

The transition from the flat, hot plains to steep, wooded mountain country is near magical. The breeze turns cool, the air clean, with a whiff of pine. Spirits lift. Dana allowed herself a few lighthearted moments as she roared up the mountain road, the wind in her face, her powerful machine sweeping her uphill effortlessly. The moment passed quickly, however. The situation she was in was disquieting and did not permit any immediate relaxation.

The battered SUV turned off the main road on to a narrow dirt track halfway up the mountain and Ashok waved to Dana, who had dropped back a little; she waved back and closed up. After a couple of kilometres the track narrowed and then petered out. The SUV stopped and the three men emerged as Dana drove up. The hillside was densely forested and the soft breeze, pine-scented and cool.

'Nice picnic spot,' observed Dana, as she parked the bike and took off her helmet. She stretched and despite the loose cotton shirt and baggy trousers that she wore, her generous figure was more than evident, as was Ashok and gang's interest in it.

'Come along, it's a short way down that path,' gestured Ashok and led the way with his cohorts. Dana slung her backpack on her shoulder and followed. A ten-minute walk led to a small clearing—quiet, remote and beautiful.

Sunlight filtered through the green canopy and the cool breeze sweeping through the pines, brought birdsong with it. The setting was picture-postcard beautiful.

'Hey, this is way better than I thought! Is it your regular party spot? It's quiet enough!' said Dana with a naughty grin. Ashok grinned back.

'This one's a player,' he thought delightedly as they all sprawled on the grass. He reached into his pocket, took out a rolled joint and offered it to Dana. 'Have some of this and then tell me how you feel.'

'Try this first,' offered Dana pulling a bottle of excellent Scotch and a mug from her backpack. She poured a generous slug into the mug for herself and handed the bottle to Ashok.

Ashok hesitated, then accepted the bottle and took a large gulp. 'This is seriously good stuff. A great change from the rotgut we drink daily. Here boys, try it—will go well with our maal.'

Chintu and Billu each took a healthy gulp and the bottle went around slowly. The trees, the breeze and the sound of the cicadas created a rather delightful ambience and the group drank in silence till the bottle was finished.

'Now let's have a smoke,' suggested Ashok. 'I'm telling you, Dana, it's great stuff, will go beautifully with the whiskey.'

Chintu, however, was always the impatient one. He sat up, turned towards Dana and said, 'Ah fuck it, bhai, enough bullshit! Let's get another taste to start off the day! Take that shirt off, baby, and let's see what you've got in there!'

Dana shook her head in disappointment. 'Now don't you go ruining a wonderful picnic. Just relax and chill.'

Chintu got to his feet and lumbered over to where Dana lay on the grass. 'Do what you are told, bitch,' he said violently. 'If I have to tear it off your tits, I'll hurt you. So do what I tell you and quickly.'

Dana took a deep breath, smiled and held out a hand as if seeking support in getting up. Chintu grabbed the proffered hand, and as he did so Dana kicked him on the right knee and with both hands yanked him down to the ground. He fell awkwardly with a yell and in that instant Dana was on her feet swinging a heavy boot very hard into his face. Chintu sprayed blood and broken teeth and Dana followed up with a carefully aimed kick to the side of his head.

She turned to Ashok, one booted foot firmly pinning the unfortunate Chintu to the ground. 'I told you I could take care of myself. Now your stupid friend has gone and ruined a perfectly good party.'

Ashok was smart and experienced, but also more than a little drunk. He got to his feet, gestured to the shocked Billu, and moved towards Dana, fumbling in his pocket for the knife he carried there. 'You fucking bitch! I'm going to cut you into little pieces now.'

Before he could complete his threat, Dana stepped forward and with a powerful leg sweep, knocked his feet out from under him. Ashok fell heavily. Dana moved up and kicked him hard on the side of his head, twice.

'You want some too, little boy?' she asked Billu, who shook his head dumbly, traumatized into silence.

'All right, flat on your face and don't move or I'll kick your brains out.'

Billu hurried to comply and Dana walked over to Chintu, who was showing some signs of recovery, and used her heavy leather boots to good effect on his head.

'Ashok Bhaiyya will kill you for this, I swear to you,' muttered Billu from his prone position, finally mustering up some courage.

'Tell Bhaiyya not to try. Next time I will kill you all, remember that.'

Dana walked back up the path to where the vehicles were parked, noted the registration number of the SUV, drew the combat knife she carried in an ankle sheath and slashed all four tires comprehensively. She then mounted hcr bikc, kick-startcd it, drovc carcfully to thc main road and resumed her journey into the mountains.

2

'These kebabs are superb,' said Sanju appreciatively, polishing off the last one remaining on the serving dish. 'Though their food quality is dropping, they still do some things really well here.'

Sanju, aka Sanjay Saran, of the Indian Police Service, was lunching at the International Centre with two of his oldest friends—tall, bulky and immensely clever Datta, who worked in the shadowy areas of 'Intelligence and Security', and Gautam Shukla, a retired colonel, who had spent years in the Army's Special Forces and now lived on a small estate deep in the interior of the Kumaon Himalayas.

'I'm sure the Centre is grateful for your kind comments, Sanju,' said Datta seriously and Gautam nodded solemnly.

'Ah, fuck off, you two,' was Sanju's reply. 'Where's the main course? They've really absorbed the geriatric bureaucratic characteristics of their principle clientele! My bhuna gosht and lehsuni naan had better not be cold or I'm sending them back, I warn you, Fatty.'

'I shall hide in the loo while you do it, Sanju,' replied Datta. 'Just give me a few seconds warning.'

Sanju just shook his head and addressed Gautam. 'Oh, by the way, Buddha, met another mountain lover the other day at one of those insufferable corporate parties that Reena insists I attend. Reena had to circulate, so I found a place at the bar and resolved to drink till she was done. Got talking to this gent, who was doing the same thing. Interesting bugger; very well informed about the hills; has a place in or near Bhimtal and shifted there two years ago with wife and cook after handing over his business to his son. The hills are really full of odd sods from the plains aren't they? People who've just upped and moved there and seem content to bugger about far from malls, hospitals, book stores and decent booze shops. Amazing eh? We discussed forestry laws and their impact on local people's rights and other "serious" social issues thereafter. Very interesting evening. Met the wife too; very well preserved and as well informed. Invited me to drop in for tea or a meal when I next came up to the hills and I might even do that on our next trip up to you, G. Anyway, how was your month-long Japanese sabbatical? Longer than your usual two-week sojourn this time eh? Gazing at your navel and no sex at all? God, how do you manage?'

Gautam smiled. 'It's tough, but after the kind of training they put one through all day, sleep is about all one is looking for, believe me!'

'So, tell me about the training, G, what were you working on?'

Gautam hesitated then answered. 'Well, karate is my basic discipline—you know I started when my mom was posted there and she bunged me into the best karate dojo she could find to keep me out of mischief.'

'Poor thing—being a busy professional and a single mom saddled with a brat like you!'

Gautam nodded. 'Yes, must have been tough. Anyway, when I spent my gap year before college at the monastery, the abbot started me off on kendo and then archery. So now I have to work on all three when I'm there. And there's always admin chores to do—kitchen work, work on the farm and so on.'

'But what about naval gazing, G? Isn't that part of the routine?'

'Of course—one has to find time for what the abbot calls "Being Quiet" or "Sitting Up".'

'The Delhi fashionistas call it Zen meditation or some such—it's all the rage, I'm told. You're not with it if you're not part of a neo-Buddhist group with chanting and meditation on weekends. What's your view on that?'

Gautam smiled and said nothing.

'Here's the food, Sanju. Now get off poor Buddha's case,' said Datta.

'Yes—he does need you to protect him, doesn't he, the great warrior san!' replied Sanju with a grin.

'Of course, I do,' replied Gautam. 'But you're looking a little off colour, Fatso. Any problem?'

Datta started on his grilled chicken and was quiet for a while. 'I have a new boss now, Buddha,' said Datta. 'And I don't think I'm going to get along with him.'

Datta's boss was the Principal Secretary to the Prime Minister.

'But what happened to old Ayengar? I didn't think he'd retire till he reached a hundred!'

'Yeah. A stroke is what happened. A minor one, but his wife put her foot down and packed him off to Chennai. He's almost eighty, for God's sake. About time he relinquished power and did some gardening—her words, not mine. The PM agreed, reluctantly, and there you have it.'

'And the new guy?'

'He's another retired bureaucrat—not as senior as Ayengar, of course, and personally honest and very hard working.'

'But?'

'Yes, but. He is a Party loyalist and very ambitious, overly so in my view, and without that fundamental sense of what I would call old-fashioned honour. I'm not sure I'm putting it very well, but that's the best I can do.'

Sanju sat back in his chair and interjected, 'Very little honour about these days, Fatso. That we've seen, haven't we?'

'Indeed, Sanju. But there used to be, if you remember. Over the last few years it's just dissipated, somehow.'

'So even if you move away, it won't help much, will it?' asked Gautam.

'No, it won't, which is why I'm toying with the idea of moving out permanently.'

Sanju sat up with a jerk. 'Good God, you want to do a Buddha, do you? Take voluntary retirement? And do what—apart from driving Annie mad.'

'Good question, as always, Sanju. And my answer is, I don't know, but I'm working on it.'

Gautam looked at his old friend thoughtfully. 'You know my offer stands, Fatso. We'll rebuild that old cottage on the edge of the estate, and you two can live in it forever more. And you can zip off for a London holiday and check on the girls whenever the peace and quiet gets too much. I'm serious and it will be great fun—you just have to make up your mind. Or rather Annie has to.'

Datta nodded but said nothing.

Sanju's cellphone buzzed, he looked at it and got up quickly.

'Got to skip dessert guys—some sort of flap going on at the office. The big chief wants me right away. We'll discuss this soon, Fatso. See you boys.'

Sanju hurried away and Gautam and Datta ordered green tea and coffee respectively. They sat in comfortable silence for a long time.

'Anything in particular bothering you, Fatso? Or is it just general dissatisfaction?'

Datta smiled. 'He's asked for the papers on both—the Bhima episode and the hunt for the Minister's assassin.'

'And?'

'And nothing, Buddha. Remember, I wrote up those files. We were monitoring Bhima from a distance, there was a mysterious explosion at his factory and an inter-gang shootout, and soon thereafter, he had a massive heart attack and died, saving us all a lot of grief. The Minister's assassin was never traced, but rumours of an expert assassin for hire faded away after that incident. Credible gangland links surfaced that established a close connection between the Honourable Minister and some very unsavory people. The Party and the powerful suddenly lost all interest in him and his untimely end. No more enquires about progress in his case. And as for the supposed assassin, underworld talk has it he died in a gang war with the Bhais—body was never found.'

'I see. Was your boss satisfied?'

'Not really, but there's nothing much he can do about it except make occasional threatening noises, which I ignore.'

'And the Big Boss?'

'He still likes me, I think. But, he's a politician. As long as I am seen to be useful, I shall survive.'

'So you must continue to be useful, Fatso.'

'Yes, or leave.'

'True. But don't brood about it for too long. Take a call. In any case, take some leave and come up to the mountains. Nothing better to clear your head than some good long walks in the hills.'

Datta nodded, signed the bill and the two friends left—Datta to go back to office and Gautam to return to Datta's house, where he was staying since his return from Japan two days ago.

3

They came late at night to deliver the message. In the interior Kumaon, nights are characterized by deep midnight blue skies ablaze with stars, and silence that is near absolute. Joshiji, whose ageing prostate had pushed him out of bed at that unearthly hour, had just finished his business in the loo when he heard the deep growl of a powerful diesel engine grinding its way up the steep incline of the kuchha road leading to the estate.

'Who is coming up here at this hour?' he muttered to himself as he pulled on a sweater, picked up his torch and shuffled to the window overlooking the gate that gave access to the property. His little cottage was located just beyond the closed-but-never-locked gate, by the side of the drive that wound almost a kilometre up the hill to the main house.

A boxy SUV, headlights ablaze, stopped at the gate; three men got out, opened the gate and walked quickly in. Joshiji had just opened his main door when the first man—tall, heavy and unshaven—barged in, grabbed him by the throat, slapped him hard and shoved him into the nearest chair.

'When is the Colonel coming back?' asked the assailant harshly. Without waiting for a reply he slapped Joshiji again, twice—forehand, backhand. Blood began dripping from Joshiji's cut lips on to his sweater. He fumbled in his pocket for a handkerchief and the man raised his hand again, but stopped as the last man to enter said in a soft but compelling voice, 'Give him a chance to answer, Jiten. Tell me, Joshiji, when is Colonel Shukla back from his trip?'

He was a tall man, slim of waist and broad of shoulder, soft voiced with grey in his hair and a commanding presence. He waited patiently as Joshiji wiped his face and repeated his question.

'When will Colonel Sahib be back, Joshiji?'

'I'm not sure,' mumbled the old man. 'Some time by the end of this week. Before Sunday, he had said.'

'Right. I've come with a message for him. But before that, I am called Pandit, God alone knows why. You might have heard some bazaar gossip about me. Have you?'

Joshiji nodded. He had indeed.

'Good, so you know I'm a serious man. Please remind the good Colonel that as I had told him about a month ago, I find this little property very attractive and will buy it at a decent price, as soon as he is back. Living alone in the mountains is no good for a retired man, you know. If an accident happens, the nearest hospital is so far away. Also, there is no Fire Brigade nearby if a sudden forest fire starts up. Tell him I'll give him a fair price, reasonably fair, in any case. And, as a reminding factor and to underline my seriousness…' he paused and nodded to his underling, 'Break one finger, please.'

Joshiji looked bewildered and then screamed as the young tough grabbed the little finger of his left hand and yanked it back till it broke.

'One more, I think, to drive the point home,' said Pandit.

Joshiji screamed again as his ring finger was broken.

'Enough for the moment. Remember, Joshiji, the Colonel will leave, but you have nowhere to go. So I can always find you when I want to. Convince your sahib, for his sake as well as yours. I'll come sometime next week to finalize the deal.'

Trembling with pain and shock, Joshiji shut the door behind Pandit and his men, swallowed two Combiflam tablets, and put his rapidly swelling and painfully throbbing hand in a bowl of cold water. He then reached for his cellphone and called his nephew, who operated a taxi service with a clapped out, fourth-hand Maruti 800, and was visiting relatives in a nearby village.

It would be a long and painful drive to the nearest hospital in Almora town.

4

Gautam and Annie were having coffee at 11 a.m., when Joshiji called and related his story.

'I have heard the name, sir. It is said he is very bad man, sir. He has killed some very big local gangsters, and is involved in many dirty things, sir—the building mafia, drugs, and even, they say, kidnapping for ransom. Nobody knows much about him and he has lots of friends in high places, it is said. I have chained the gate, sir, and Raju and Pratap are guarding it in twelve hour shifts, sir. When will you be coming up?'

Gautam thought quickly. 'I'll leave tonight—around twelve to avoid the traffic. I'll talk to you from Haldwani and when I pass Almora. Tell the boys to be alert for fire, but not to get into any dhakka-mukki with anyone. Keep yourselves safe. I'll deal with this.'

Gautam poured himself another cup of coffee and related the details of Joshiji's nasty encounter to a horrified Annie.

'I thought the hills were free of hard core crime, Buddha! This sounds like the wilds of Bihar or some such!'

Gautam shook his head. 'I admit I'm a little shocked, Annie, and angry with myself for not having foreseen this. You see, the day I was leaving for Japan—I had checked in for the flight and was waiting to board—this fellow, Pandit, called me and said he was coming to meet me. When I told him I was about to board a flight to go abroad and would be back only after a month, he gave me his spiel on phone—he wanted to buy my place, would give me a decent price and would like to warn me of the dangers of living alone in such a lonely spot, far from hospitals and policemen. He elaborated his threats and I brushed him off with some guff about thinking on his proposition and deciding on my return. I didn't realize he would leave a message for me in this fashion on my return. Also, it takes a special sort of human being to hurt an old man like this.'

'Now don't you get all heroic and go solo into this mess, G. Let's discuss this with Datta and Sanju, and work out a plan. I'll call Sanju over for dinner—Reena is out of town on work as usual.'

Gautam laughed. 'I'm way past the age of heroism, Annie. But this stuff has to be dealt with quickly and firmly, else it gets out of hand.'

'Yes, of course. Anyway, I'm glad you are not losing it, G—or, as usual, not showing it, to stop me worrying! Let's go to Khan Market—I have a lot of shopping to do. And you can do some of it for me. They take one look at my angrezi skin and eye colour and double their frikking prices. And all this despite my fluent, accent-less Hindi and Punjabi!'

Gautam laughed again. 'Can't blame them, Annie. White foreigners have lotsa dollars don't they? They can afford higher prices!'

'This white Indian citizen doesn't and cannot G! And the logic doesn't hold in reverse. They don't add to my salary at the University because of my bloody ethnicity!

Anyway, enough about me. Tell me when is Ruth back from her…training programme, was it?'

'Not sure, Annie, but should be soon. At least, that's what her last mail indicated.'

Annie nodded, hesitated imperceptibly, and said, 'This one is a keeper, G, but it won't be easy, for either of you. So what are you thinking of doing, if I may ask.'

No one but Annie would have asked such a question of Gautam and she was the only one Gautam would give a reply to.

Gautam smiled in response, and Annie saw a touch of melancholy alongside the affection that was shared between them.

'I agree, Annie, it's real and I don't know where it will end. All I know is, I don't want it to. Let's see what is in store for us. Come on, your ladyship, your chariot awaits.'

Annie picked up a couple of voluminous shopping bags and Gautam drove her to the market in his red Gypsy.

~

The friends sat down with coffee after an early dinner and Annie broke the long silence. 'Must you rush off immediately, Buddha? Let Sanju and Datta find out who these guys are, get some intel before you jump in, breathing fire and brimstone.'

Gautam smiled. 'That will take time, Annie, and I don't want my people hurt any more or the place burnt down. Don't worry, I'm not jumping into anything without looking at all the risks and available options. But I must be there, not away.'

'You are protesting too much, G, and that worries me.'

Sanju nodded agreement. 'Yes, just go slow, bro, till the picture is clear. What surprises me, however, is the barefaced confidence of this gang. We are a society of connections—how do they know what your connections are with local officialdom and politicians?'

'Perhaps, they do know that I have no important local connections. Shows the extent of their local knowledge and the strength of their local contacts.'

'True, true. You're very quiet, Fatso, what's up?'

'I'm thinking—you should try it sometime, Sanju, it's a useful thing.'

'Oh, the fat man is getting nasty—means he's worried. Why are you worried, Fatty? You think Buddha here can't handle a bunch of local wannabe thugs?'

Datta shook his head impatiently. 'I'm sure Buddha can scare off a bunch of hoodlums easily enough, but is that what these fellows are? Local toughs trying their luck with a bit of extortion from a well-off "outsider"? If they are more than that, then we have trouble. G wants a quiet, retired life—not stories about gun-battles in the quiet Kumaon countryside in the local newspapers and questions in the state legislature. Let me tap a few official sources for more info. You do the same, Sanju, and we'll pool our info and see how to tackle this.'

'And I can send some reinforcements immediately, G. Our Israeli partner is in the mountains on a biking holiday. I'll ask her to come to your place ASAP and you can plan your defenses—or with her around, I should say "offenses".'

Gautam laughed, 'Don't disrupt her holiday right away, Sanju. Just tell her that I'll call if necessary. Let me assess the situation on the ground first. And now guys, I'm off to catch a few hours of sleep before I leave around twelve o'clock.'

'I'll knock at eleven-forty-five, Buddha—you know that's early for me,' said Annie.

'It's late for me, so bye for now, G, we'll talk tomorrow afternoon, after you get home and take a look around,' added Datta and the party broke up.

Around noon the next day, the man known as Pandit received a call on his cellphone.

'Colonel Sahib drove past in his red Gypsy some time ago—should have reached home by now.'

'Good. Keep a watch,' replied Pandit and disconnected.

'We will let him stew for a few days,' said Pandit to himself. 'Then go over and finalize the deal.'

He then dialed a Delhi number and informed an interested party that the property he had liked would soon be available and he should get the money together and be prepared to drive up at very short notice.

'Remember, I won't hold it for you—many others have expressed a serious interest in it. So be ready to come when I call, else you lose it.'

The customer's response was, however, disconcerting. Pandit had sent him details of the property from the land records and photographs from the ridge overlooking the estate, and since he had liked what he saw, the customer had done some research on Colonel (retired) Gautam Shukla, using government sources. The results were a trifle worrying.

'Don't worry, sirji, I have dealt with all sorts of people and I will deal with this colonel sahib also. You relax and make arrangements for the money; I will look after matters at this end.'

Despite the confident tone he had adopted on phone, Pandit was uneasy and after some thought made a series of calls to Delhi, Dehradun and Nainital and set enquiries in motion.

'Must meet this Shukla face to face and assess the situation myself,' he muttered to himself and put the matter aside for the moment. His businesses were expanding, and he had other issues to sort out on an urgent basis.

Dana was on her way back to the Kumaon Mandal Vikas Nigam Tourist Rest House in Munsiyari from a short limbering-up trek when Sanju called.

'I know an excellent little place within an hour's drive of Colonel Shukla's estate. One of those well-run "village home stays"—an independent little hut with a modern loo and a well-equipped kitchenette. I'll be there by noon tomorrow, by which time the Colonel will have assessed the situation on the ground. We'll talk and decide on the next steps then.'

'Excellent,' said Sanju. 'I'll call you tomorrow, after talking to Buddha.'

'Great,' said Dana and before disconnecting informed Sanju about her encounter with Ashok and gang and gave him the registration number of the SUV.

Sanju laughed. 'Hope they learn a lesson, Dana. I'll trace the vehicle as a matter of course and keep records. We might want to visit them again—can't have garbage like this running around having their wicked way with people. Anyway, take care of yourself,' said Sanju and ended the call.

5

Gautam reached home by 11 a.m. to find his entire staff waiting to receive him. Even the cook, not given to social niceties, came out, sketched Gautam a salute and took charge of the two dogs, who had spent the month in Delhi being spoiled rotten by Annie. The dogs, their metal 'leopard collars' fixed round their necks, raced off to reacquaint themselves with every tree, bush and creature on the estate.

Gautam examined Joshiji's splinted fingers, noted the swelling on his lips and asked the elderly estate manager for complete details of Pandit's nocturnal visit. He listened to Joshiji's detailed and animated description of the night's visitors and events in complete silence and when the old man had finished, just gripped his shoulder for a long moment.

'You have been very brave, Joshiji,' he said gently. 'I have no words to praise or thank you for your commitment, but I'll never forget this.'

He then went into the house and after a quick wash and a cup of tea set off to inspect the firefighting readiness of his estate. The inspection lasted two hours and was generally satisfactory.

Gradually the magic of the mountains had its effect on Gautam, as it always did. The silence, the breeze, the rolling vistas quietened him. Suddenly, from way down the hill, a flute began to play a haunting, old, folk ditty. Gautam stopped to listen to the music and quietly revel in the wonder of it all. He then shook his head to break the spell and went down to the house.

'And they want to take this away from me by force,' he said, struggling to contain the wave of fury that threatened to overwhelm him.

Joshiji was waiting outside the house, concerned at the strange, very disturbing look on his master's face.

'We need to clear all the undergrowth from the firebreaks, Joshiji. Get the boys on that and I'll join them after lunch. We must have it clear by end of day tomorrow.'

The two lads from the village that were part of the permanent staff started work, while Gautam tested the pumps at the three water storage tanks on the estate and checked the hoses kept for firefighting. Finding things in more-or-less good order, Gautam got down to work with the boys and by evening a good bit of cleaning up was done.

'Give the boys food and let them sleep for a few hours, Joshiji. I'll keep watch till midnight and then wake them up,' said Gautam. 'The dogs will, of course, give us a warning of anything untoward.'

The night passed without incident. A hard day's work later, the firebreaks were clear. Gautam repeated the previous night's pattern—he kept watch till midnight and then the boys came on duty.

After morning tea, Gautam dismissed the lads. 'Go home, get some rest and be back by seven. We'll suspend normal work on the estate for now—just keep a fire watch at night for some time.'

'We have trouble, Datta,' said Sanju sprawling in one of the two armchairs set across from the sofa in Datta's office. 'This Pandit character eyeing Buddha's estate is a new, reportedly very rough, crook operating in the Kumaon districts. Lives in the shadows—even my people, who are well up on the underworld, don't have anything much on him, except that he's apparently not very young, uses teams of young toughs and occasionally does some strong arm work himself to keep his boys suitably in awe of him. Very well connected—politically and otherwise. I'm twisting some arms for more info. Let's see what we get, but I'm not feeling very easy. I called Buddha and told him to be careful, but you know how he gets when he's seriously angry—all quiet and monosyllabic.'

Datta nodded. 'Yes. These guys hurting Joshiji has really pissed him off and that worries me. Remember these are locals—not outsiders. Local connections make for local repercussions—and that's not good if you plan to live there in retirement.'

'Yup, I get your point, but you can't be driven out of home and hearth and just accept it for fear of repercussions locally. Not if you are friend Buddha, you don't.'

'Very true. Especially now that he's really angry. Besides, we don't have official backing and my boss has no relationship with Buddha, the way old Ayengar had. I can't use official clout to cover up mayhem in the countryside like we did earlier.'

'We'd better advise Buddha to keep it quiet then—no public confrontations, no witnesses, no noise.'

'Yes. I'll talk to him tonight. He's been checking up his firefighting equipment and infrastructure. The water tanks are all full, the pumps are working and his two boys from the village are staying on the estate on fire watch at night. Joshiji has had his broken fingers splinted up and is back on site and the cook, Gautam tells me, has been sharpening his khukri. That old Gurkha is far more dangerous than the village lads, despite being in his sixties.'

'Old Bahadur does make a mean omelette, but what makes him dangerous outside the kitchen?' asked Sanju.

'Old Sher Bahadur Thapa served with Buddha in his Special Forces unit. He was invalidated out after he took two bullets in the leg when they were in Sri Lanka, years ago. Gautam sent him to some cookery school and set him up as his cook at the estate. Educated his two sons. Bright boys—one's a captain in the Paras and the older one is an engineer with some big construction company. Wife died back home in Nepal when he was still in active service with G somewhere in the wilds. Anyway, I would be careful of Sher Bahadur if I were a bad guy going up against Buddha.'

'Whoops! I didn't know any of this!' remarked Sanju.

'Neither did I,' replied Datta. 'Annie got it out of the old man when we were last up there. She spent time in the kitchen teaching him some pastry recipes and fishing out the secrets of his mutton biryani. He talked to her—most people do when Annie decides to become friends.'

'Yes, Annie does have the knack. Anyway, I've activated Dana and also informed the Israelis at Tinauli that I might need their help. They were very positive and will visit G very soon—within a day or two. That's about all we can do at this point.'

'It's a lot, Sanju. Annie and I were thinking of paying G a visit—take a crate of wine along and make a picnic of it—but until he sorts this mess out, I don't think he'll want us around.

'Yeah, let things get straightened out first. Can't put the women in harm's way if it's a bad sort of scene.'

'Ok. Once G resolves this issue and gives a go-ahead, we'll drive up. Start working on your boss—persuade him that the universe will continue to roll along in your absence.'

Sanju grinned and got up to go. 'Don't be nasty now. My boss is just another insecure bureaucrat nearing retirement, bless his soul. I'll persuade him—I trust. I'll talk to you tomorrow.'

6

Village Tinauli was located below the ridge across the valley from Gautam's estate. Getting to it involved trekking for a total of about four hours: down to the valley floor, across the river, up the hill to the ridge line and down a short distance on the other side. The young people of the village had all moved away to the plains years ago; the village had ample water but it had neither school nor jobs, not even a motorable road—and the elders were left behind to make do with some remitted money and limited makeshift agriculture.

Then, about a decade ago, four Israelis had settled there—an elderly couple, Deborah and Reuben, and two much younger men, Yaakov and Ben. The young men soon found partners locally, and much to the astonishment of the few remaining villagers, settled down to quiet domesticity. The foreigners were very good agriculturists, and the almost-abandoned village soon began yielding an excellent income from vegetables, fruit, poultry and dairy, not only for the foreigners, but also for the remaining villagers who leased their lands to them.

But the mountains didn't remain peaceful for long. An attempt by a powerful drug cartel to set up opium poppy cultivation in abandoned villages like Tinauli had attracted Gautam's attention, and the subsequent violent confrontation involved the Tinauli Israelis, who worked with him and his 'official' partners against the Narcos.

Sanju's call to Deborah, the alpha of the group, led to the two elders starting off early morning from Tinauli, two days after Gautam had returned. They took a detour to his place, skirting the village cluster of which his estate was formally a part.

Coffee was served, lunch ordered and the three sat down to talk.

'This Pandit fellow has a bad reputation, Gautam,' observed Deborah. 'We made some enquiries and the reaction was uniformly negative. People know very little and say less—they are seriously afraid to talk. But we did get some data—after all we are locals with strong economic ties to people in the area.'

Gautam smiled and poured more coffee.

'He has several places where he and his teams hang out. The HQ is supposedly somewhere in the Bhimtal-Bhowali area—hiding in plain sight, perhaps—hangouts in the Berinag area, and establishments in the terai in the Ramnagar-Haldwani region. He runs much of the smuggling out of the interior via Ranikhet-Ramnagar, has abducted a couple of rich builders for ransom and yes, is believed to have gone into property dealing recently.'

Gautam nodded appreciatively. 'For all your isolation, you have good sources of information.'

'The boys travel a lot and speak the local language fluently now, and that helps. I just sit around and listen to all their gossip,' Deborah replied. 'I've sent Ben out to get more details—he's the outgoing, social one with a hundred friends, from bus conductors to hotel owners. He'll wander around and pick up snippets that we'll weave a picture from. Meanwhile, I'll have Yaakov do a recce of your area—see if they've set up watchers around here. Once we know where they are and how they work, it'll be easy to take them out whenever we want.'

'I'm extremely grateful for all the trouble you people are taking. But please be careful—no point in calling attention to yourselves. These are nasty people obviously. Tell your boys not to get too close—it's not worth the risk.'

Reuben laughed. 'Things were getting a little too comfortable, Colonel. A shot of adrenalin will do us all good. And don't worry, we don't take unnecessary risks, but we do have to protect what we have built from people like this.'

The cook announced lunch and the conversation shifted to water conservation, poly-house construction and dairy farming. Soon after lunch, the Israeli couple left and Gautam went on a recee of his own in the forest that more or less surrounded his little estate.

Gautam had, over the years, familiarized himself with the myriad footpaths that threaded the forest and a detailed, careful reconnaissance showed that there were no strange and unwanted humans in the area as yet. A year ago, a female leopard had made her den in a shallow cave in the thick forest and had given birth to two cubs. Gautam's staff had told him about it and for several months the area had been given a wide berth by everyone—nobody wanted to tackle a new mother bringing up her young! It was only when the boys reported that apparently the cat family had vacated the premises that grass cutting, wood-gathering and other routine tasks recommenced in the area. One or more leopards did occasionally visit the area—the dogs went ballistic when they did—and Gautam noticed some fresh pug marks when he did his walkabout.

'Scare any intruders away, guys,' said Gautam addressing the forest, which had flourished since Gautam's grandfather had begun looking after it.

'Prevent indiscriminate tree felling, stop forest fires as soon as they start, and leave the jungle alone. Just do this and the forest will regenerate remarkably fast,' his grandfather had said, and the old man knew what he was talking about. He had turned a barren, almost treeless ridge into a flourishing oak forest in the thirty years he had spent in his Himalayan refuge and Gautam had every intention of continuing the tradition.

Gautam stopped near the ridge line, stepped up on a large rock that jutted out of the mountainside and looked downhill. A thin thread of smoke rose from his kitchen chimney, the only sign of human presence, as the trees hid the house completely from this particular location. The sunlight seeping through the tree cover dappled the greens with yellow and the only sound was that of a slight breeze ruffling the oak leaves. For a long moment Gautam savoured the silence; then he turned and made his way back down the mountainside.

After the meeting with the Israelis, two days passed quietly. On the third day, Pandit and his cohorts came visiting in the late morning. They came in a dusty but new Scorpio and as they drove up the narrow, twisting, kuchcha road to the estate, Gautam could hear the diesel grinding its way uphill. He walked down to his gate, chained and locked at all times since Pandit's last visit, unlocked it, went out, locked it behind him and stood waiting.

'What the fuck?' exclaimed Pandit's driver, as they rounded the last bend and saw Gautam standing in front of the gate. What they saw was a slim man of medium height, dressed in track pants, tee-shirt and a light fleece jacket with grey trainers on his feet, bareheaded and totally relaxed.

'Shall I speed up and give him a serious scare, boss?' asked the driver.

'Yes, but don't run him over. If he is Gautam Shukla, I don't want him dead before he signs the sale deed.'

'Not to worry, boss. I know how to do this,' the driver replied and tramped down on the accelerator. The engine roared and the Scorpio surged forward, menacingly.

Gautam stood his ground. The noise of the straining diesel was loud, but the gradient and the kuchcha track limited the speed, and Gautam had assessed at what point he would have to take evasive action.

'Move fucker,' grunted the driver as the vehicle surged towards the still figure standing hands on hips, apparently without a care in the world.

As the SUV approached, Gautam held up his left hand in the universal 'STOP' signal.

The vehicle came on.

'Careful,' said Pandit warningly, and the driver slammed on the brakes.

Gautam took a deep breath—another two metres and he would have had to jump aside and run around to outflank the big SUV.

The vehicle skidded a little and stopped.

'Stay in the vehicle, you two,' said Pandit, as he opened the door and stepped out.

'Colonel Shukla?' he queried as he walked towards Gautam, who only nodded.

Pandit stepped up close, trying to intimidate Gautam with his taller frame.

'I am Pandit and I had left a message for you with your manager.'

Gautam nodded again.

'I have the papers here, Colonel Sahib, for you to sign, and I'm offering you a fairly decent price. You can, of course, tough it out and say no, but that would be unwise. Your two staff from the village will not be coming to work anymore. They have family here—wives, children, parents, siblings—and they've been told what will happen if they come back. And you, too, have to step out sometime. Our hill roads are narrow and can be very dangerous. Besides, it's not as if you have an impregnable fortress here. And the nearest hospital is far away. So, you have to make up your mind, Colonel, and quickly. I understand you have been some sort of commando or something, but you are alone here and I have any number of people available. You cannot win, and my price falls as time passes.'

Pandit paused and Gautam kept a poker face, firmly repressed a rising wave of fury, and asked, 'Why did you hurt Joshiji? He's an old man, he doesn't deserve this.'

'Oh, just to emphasize the fact that I'm serious and I'll seriously hurt you and any and all associated with you if you don't do as I say. As simple as that, Colonel Sa'ab, and as serious. So, what's your answer?'

Gautam took a deep breath, paused for a while then nodded reluctantly.

'I don't really have a choice, do I? There's no other course of action. But I need some time to pack and move all my personal stuff, so you'll have to wait for a while, say fifteen days. I'll get packers from Delhi and move out in two weeks' time; I'll sign the papers then. And I'll need the boys from the village to help—so you will have to arrange that.'

Pandit shook his head appreciatively. 'Yes, they did say you have some balls on you! Trying to set conditions when you have no leverage available. Or, do you think you'll make a few calls to friends in Delhi and use some influence here? Won't work, Colonel Sa'ab, just won't work. And if you are stupid enough to try, there will be repercussions, serious repercussions, you understand me?'

'I understand and I realize that Delhi is too far away. Besides, I really don't have that level of "influence" anyway. But I do need the time.'

'Ok,' replied Pandit after some thought. 'I have some urgent business to deal with, so you get ten days to pack. Then I'll be back. And no more conversation, you hear. You sign, take your money and leave, or else we break your knees and you sign in hospital.'

Pandit got into his SUV and left.

Gautam stood still for a long time, looking at the play of light and shade on the mountains and valleys stretching away to the horizon: the landscape that had bewitched him from early childhood. A Himalayan barbet called incessantly from somewhere high up in the oak forest, a soft breeze ruffled his hair. Finally, he turned, opened the gate, and locking it behind him walked slowly back to the house.

Joshiji, waiting worriedly on the porch, stepped forward to ask questions, then quickly stepped back in silence. Gautam went into the house without a word and Joshiji walked down to his cottage wondering why the quiet, almost serene, expression on his master's face had evoked a frisson of fear in his heart.

~

After lunch, Gautam went walkabout on the ridge above his house. This time however, he had specific objectives in mind. Having earmarked certain locations, he tried calling Tinauli, but cellphone connectivity was iffy at the best of times and he didn't get through.

'You'd better get there tomorrow, old fellow,' he said to himself as he walked back to the house. 'The walk will do you good.'

He entered the house to find Sher Bahadur pottering about in the dining room.

'You are preparing for trouble, Sher Bahadur,' said Gautam, as he noticed the khukri on the old Gurkha's belt.

The old soldier nodded. 'Always, sahib,' he replied, ever a man of few words.

'A gun perhaps, now?' asked Sher Bahadur.

'When needed, not now,' replied Gautam and turned away.

Sher Bahadur shook his head slightly and returned to the kitchen.

~

Gautam left early the next morning, set a demanding pace and was in Tinauli before twelve. He related the essence of his conversation with Pandit to the four Israelis, over tea on Deborah's porch.

'If you folks are willing to get involved, I have a plan

to deal with this situation. And I'll try and ensure none of you gets up close with this lot either.'

Deborah smiled. 'All of us have been up against the sharp end, Colonel, and we owe you, so please don't get so protective all of a sudden. We are at your disposal for anything that you need any of us for.'

Gautam nodded. 'Thank you for this, all of you. I will need these young men here, Deborah, for what I see as essentially a surveillance operation. However, as we all know how fast shit can hit the fan, I'll provide the hardware they need, just in case.'

Gautam outlined his plan quickly; they finalized the broad contours over lunch and he left soon thereafter.

'You boys had better go check up your bikes,' suggested Deborah. 'Your worthy brothers-in-law are not very strong on maintenance, are they?'

Yaakov and Ben grinned. Their Indian partners' families were delighted to have the use of two high-end motorcycles parked in their village, five miles down the road from Gautam, but were careless about maintenance in any form.

'No, Deb, they sure aren't,' replied Yaakov. 'We'll go down tomorrow and service them. Can't let the Colonel down at the last minute.'

7

The Principle Private Secretary to the Prime Minister, Dr Shashi Bhushan Mathur, summoned Datta to his office after lunch and offered him a chair and tea. Datta shifted mental gears to high alert. Such politenesses were uncommon with the PPS, known for his distant attitude—some called it cold and arrogant—in dealing with juniors and other 'unimportant' people.

When tea was served and they had the room to themselves, Shri Mathur cleared his throat, took a sip and opened the conversation.

'Someone from the French Embassy met me a month ago—the Chargé d'affaires, along with their Security person—you probably know him.'

Datta nodded.

'They came with a problem, a serious one, and asked for help.'

Shri Mathur took another sip, set the cup down and took a deep, decisive breath. 'The daughter of a major French industrialist went trekking in the Kumaon with her boyfriend, also French, and they haven't been heard of for almost a month. The father is close to the present regime in Paris and asked the President's office for help. They play golf together—the French President and the father. Anyway, the upshot was that I advised the Embassy people to follow protocol, and go through the External Affairs people to the Home Ministry. I spoke to the Home Secretary, who asked the Uttarakhand Government, who traced the young couple to Munsiyari, where they stayed at the KMVN Tourist Rest House and the manager there reported that they mentioned plans of going trekking into the high Himalayas. Nobody knew any more details of their itinerary. They paid their bills and set off one morning and have not been seen since. The local police have done a fair amount of work apparently, questioning people—taxi drivers, bus drivers, other trekkers in the area and so on—but have as yet got nowhere. They haven't finished, but, from what I can gather from my contacts, they have more or less exhausted all possibilities, and barring a miracle, will soon submit a report saying the couple cannot be traced. If that happens the French will come back to me and I will hand them over to you.'

Shri Mathur sipped some more tea and waited for Datta's reaction.

Finishing the last of his tea, Datta put the cup down, waited a few seconds and responded. 'I'm not sure how I can help, sir. This sort of problem requires the resources of a large, well-organized police force. I do not have such resources.'

'A large, well-organized police force has already tried and failed. We now need something different, a different approach. We have nothing else.'

'We can simply tell the French that we tried and failed, sir. They are not going to cancel the defense contracts because of this. They have to sell their stuff just as much as we need to buy it.'

'I am well aware of that, Datta,' replied the PPS, a touch of irritation in his voice. 'But we still need to take one last shot, however much of a long shot it may be. I do realize the difficulties, but your unorthodox methods and off the book assets sometimes get results. We must make one last effort and then, if it doesn't work, we can tell them we tried everything we could. Please initiate immediate action. You can use funds and resources from the Bureau and that includes your friend Saran. I have told the Director that Saran will be working with you exclusively on this case.'

Shri Mathur leaned back in his chair and allowed his lips to twitch in a small semblance of a smile.

'I do try to keep abreast of important events, despite the very slim files that you seem to maintain on them, Datta. I still do not approve of "black" operations, but sometimes they work, and exceptions are sometimes necessary to prove the rules. The matter is urgent, so please set things in motion immediately. And let me know when you have something of significance.'

Datta got up and left as the PPS picked up a file from his in-tray, opened it and began to read.

8

'This is absurd, Fatso,' protested Sanju. 'We do not have the manpower to go hunting all over the Kumaon for lost foreigners, and you know it.'

It was late evening, and Sanju and Datta were ensconced in Datta's study waiting for Annie to announce dinner.

'I know, Sanju, I know,' said Datta 'But what you don't know is the politics behind this. The ostensible reason for this absurdity is that the French are major partners in defense and economic affairs and so we will do everything possible—orthodox and otherwise—to resolve any problems that arise. The real reason is that old Mathur's daughter is just winding up a PhD at the Sorbonne and is looking to find a job and settle down in *Paree* with her French boyfriend; hence the concern and the last-ditch, though obviously doomed, attempt. The French will call me when the Home Ministry admits defeat and my boss points them in my direction, and I'll hold a meeting with them and you, get all the details and start our efforts to find this missing couple. Everyone's covering their arse—if we succeed, everyone shares in the glory, if we fail, Indians are known to be sloppy anyway. It's a win-win for everyone except us, of course, but we don't matter.'

Sanju nodded and reached for the bottle of Ardbeg that Datta had opened on his arrival.

'So, what do you want us to do?'

'What we always do, Sanju, our best, despite the constraints. Look, if they had got into an accident or simply checked into some ashram to find the meaning of life or are shacked up in a village stoned out of their minds, the cops would have found them. I spoke to everyone who matters in officialdom and their reports are detailed—they put in a lot of work on this. So, it's not a routine disappearance. Of course, if they seriously want to disappear, it's a large country, but if there's some dirty work afoot, perhaps we can have a go at some informal investigation.'

Sanju reached for the bowl of peanuts and took a handful. 'Dana is tied up with Buddha and his mess otherwise…' Sanju's voice trailed off and he sat in silence for a while.

'What happened there, Sanju? Did you actually have a thought strike you?' asked Datta when Sanju finally sat up from his near horizontal position on the couch and reached for his glass.

Sanju grinned. 'Yes, O Great Sage, but I need to dig a bit to see where it goes. Anyway, I'll talk to my Pahari boys and chalk out a course of action. Now I'm off to investigate the kitchen for the biryani that Annie had promised me.'

9

Pandit grabbed the hapless Billu by the throat and almost effortlessly hoisted him till he was teetering on his toes trying desperately to breathe and not succeeding very well.

'Tell me the whole story, you little bastard, before I throttle you and toss your carcass into the ravine for the wild boars. Every word, from the time you saw the woman till she kicked your sorry arses and walked away. Now!'

The young tough crumpled to his knees and croaked out a comprehensive account of their encounter with Dana. When he fell silent, Pandit turned to Ashok and looked at him quizzically. 'One of my top teams taken apart by one woman! No wonder you didn't have the balls to tell me the whole story. And you thought I wouldn't be able to tell bullshit from fact. That was your second mistake—not telling me the truth. Now what should I do with you?'

Pandit's voice was soft and speculative, almost gentle, and it terrified Ashok. He knew the big man was teetering on the edge of a murderous rage and he just bowed his head and waited without saying a word. His silence probably helped, because after a long, quiet moment, Pandit drew a deep breath and turned away to look out of the window.

'You have worked well all this while, Ashok, but this is a major fuck up. One man in hospital and you two pricks looking like something my dog Bholu vomited up. You are obviously unfit for active duty and you are lucky I have a need for some shit-brained idiots to do guard duty for a while. You will go to our place near Berinag, relieve Mintu Mobile and his boys, and stay and guard the white couple we have there. And remember they are business goods of high value and are not to be damaged in any way. Keep your prick in your pants or I'll cut it off and shove it down your throat—and I'm not joking here, you know that?'

Ashok nodded. Pandit was fully capable of doing exactly what he said he would.

'Now get your fucking faces out of my sight.'

Ashok and Billu quickly left the room. Pandit called for tea, sat down in his favourite armchair, picked up his cellphone and made a call.

'Guddu, get a clean phone, call the French number I gave you, ask for the man whose name I can't pronounce but you can, and tell him we have his daughter and her boyfriend. He's sweated long enough, I think, and will be ready to talk business. Tell him we want one million dollars at today's exchange rate. And send him the video of the couple that I sent you. Keep it very short and professional. Say you'll call back and disconnect and throw away the phone. Get a fresh phone and call them again tomorrow. Ask them if they agree to the ransom and once they agree, and they will, for sure, tell them to get the money to India and be ready for an exchange. We will contact them in a week's time, so that's how much time they have to get their act together. Let me know what they say and get rid of the phone after the conversation. Make sure you don't fuck this up, Guddu. Get this done properly.'

Tea was served and Pandit took a contented sip. Things were going well, business was good.

10

'It's no longer a disappearance, Datta, it's a kidnapping,' said Mr Mathur crisply. 'The French officials will be in your office shortly and now it's entirely your baby. I don't want the flatfoots involved in this; you can have all the resources you need, just get this sorted quickly. The French couple back to Daddy in one piece, yesterday, if possible.'

The PPS to the PM disconnected and Datta buzzed Sanju and asked him to come over.

Sanju arrived in fifteen minutes, the French in an hour.

'There have been important developments, Mr Datta,' said the French Chargé d'affaires. 'Jean Pierre here will give us the details.'

The security officer, Jean Pierre, who was accompanied by a colleague—an elegant, very quiet and not so young lady—fished out a sheet of paper and a memory stick from his briefcase, and began.

'The father of the girl has received a ransom demand. One million dollars—at a given exchange rate—for the safe return of the couple, completely unharmed. A video of the couple reading a two-day old newspaper was also mailed to the father. A day later, they called back to confirm the father's willingness to pay the ransom and said that the money should be arranged and the exchange will take place after a week. All this from different cellphones, details of which our tech people have put on this memory stick. You may like to investigate further. As you are aware, the girl's father is a close friend of the President and so, Madame Defarge here,' he nodded towards the lady accompanying him, 'was deputed, with an associate who will be arriving later today, to come here to coordinate with your people and sort out the matter.'

'You've moved very quickly,' observed Datta, looking not at Jean Pierre but at the lady accompanying him, who looked down at her hands, folded neatly in her lap, and did not reply.

Jean Pierre continued, 'They were, of course, told that the ransom will be paid subject to proof of life. They were also told that it would take time to organize things in far-away India. They replied that they would send the details for the exchange—cash for the couple—when they called next, and we, the father and his people, must finalize arrangements and be ready very quickly. They were precise—said we should be ready within a week and that the exchange will be scheduled any day thereafter and no changes will be accepted. The video and other data is on this stick and the sequence of events is detailed on this sheet.' He handed the paper and the memory stick to Datta and sat back.

The Chargé d'affaires cleared his throat and got to his feet. 'I think I'll leave you all to discuss the details of further action to be taken, Mr Datta. Please be assured of all assistance from us—all our resources are available to resolve this unfortunate matter.'

As the senior diplomat left the room, Datta looked up at the lady sitting beside Jean Pierre and smiled. 'Welcome,

Madame, er, Defarge, was it? What a delightfully Dickensian touch that adds to the situation. And what is your remit from your chief, in this matter?'

Madame Defarge looked puzzled. 'I'm not sure I understand what you are saying.'

Datta sighed and looked at Sanju, who fished out a sheet of paper from his pocket and began to read. 'Passport in the name of Thérèse Defarge, arrived yesterday from Paris, senior officer in the Directorate General of Internal Security; degrees in Arabic and Middle Eastern History from the Sorbonne, extensive experience in counter terrorism…' Sanju paused and looked at Datta. 'Do I need to go on?'

Datta smiled and shook his head. 'Things would go well if we were a trifle open with each other, Madame. Distrust makes for inefficiency and we don't want any mess-ups here, do we?'

Madame Defarge smiled back and with a slight shake of her head and subtle change of posture, was suddenly transformed from a mousy underling to a quietly confident personage very much in a leadership role.

'I'm very happy to see you live up to your reputation, sir. It makes my job so much easier.'

'And what exactly is your job here, Madame?' asked Datta.

'To get the young people back safe and sound, of course. The President, as you know, is personally concerned in this—the girl is like a favourite niece. The money is ready—in small notes as instructed—and we are waiting for further instructions from the kidnappers.'

Datta nodded. 'Just to get things clear from the outset, Madame. You do not get to execute secret ops here; we will do whatever is necessary.'

'I am happy to hand over control to you, Mr Datta. Your reputation precedes you, as I said, all the way to Paris. I would, however, request that we be allowed to work with your team. After all, you don't want to treat different allies differently, do you?' said Madame, with a slight smile.

Datta shook his head in mock sorrow and looked at Sanju. 'And this is the secret world, Mr Saran, where everyone seems to know everything about everyone! Ironic isn't it.'

Sanju smiled and said nothing.

Datta continued. 'Mr Saran here will be in-charge of the…um…project and all executive action needed will be under his supervision. He is setting up a command post in a safe house and we should meet there hereafter, starting this afternoon. All yours, Sanju.'

'Thank you, Datta. Please call me Sanjay, people, we are not fixated on formalities here.'

He handed a slip of paper to Madame Defarge. 'This is the address and I would recommend you use vehicles with local number plates, not diplomatic ones. If you have any problems there, we can provide vehicles for you. Bring your team along so we can meet and set up some protocols for communication and future action. If you need local numbers for your cellphones, we can provide the necessary SIM cards. Let us meet at 3.30 p.m. and talk further. I have to get some things done by then, so I'll be off.'

Madame Defarge nodded. 'Please call me Didi—this Madame bit makes me feel old—and Jean Pierre remains Jean Pierre. We will see you at 3.30, Sanjay, thank you.'

Sanju left and the French also got up to go.

'I need to get back to the Embassy to see if anything new has occurred. Shall we see you at the safe house, Mr Datta?'

'Oh, just Datta, please. Everyone calls me that. And yes, of course—if I can get away. But this issue is my principle concern for the moment, and I will be in touch with Sanju,' replied Datta and showed the visitors out.

After meeting with the French in Datta's office, Sanju called Dana.

'Do you think the gang that tried to act smart with you could be linked to this French tourist abduction? That would be classical synchronicity!'

Dana thought for a while before answering. 'It would be quite a coincidence, wouldn't it? But then the French couple also started into the Kumaon from Haldwani and these people were working as a gang—quite well organized. And the leader, Ashok, was good with his approach—very professional. Came across as rough, but not frightening—at least to inexperienced young people. Just the right type to score some charas and ganja from, if that's what you were looking for.'

'My gut is telling me to explore this lead—whatever it may be worth,' responded Sanju. 'The SUV is registered to one Ashok Tyagi and the address is a farmhouse in the Haldwani-Rudrapur area. Why don't you drive down and check out this address, carefully and from a distance, Dana! If Ashok and company are there, I'll send you backup and then you can grab them and question them a little intensively. What are you carrying, by the way?'

'Just my knives and the handgun you got me a license for. Should be enough.'

'For now, yes. But if you have to take over the

farmhouse, I'll send some stuff with your backup; it will probably be Bhanu Bisht. You haven't met him, but he's good. Has a lot of combat experience, but not in a "civilian environment". Anyway, that's for later. Can you be in Haldwani by nightfall?'

'Sure. I'm near Berinag—should take me about seven hours to get to Haldwani, if I drive carefully. I'll pass quite close to the Colonel's place in the Jhaltola area en route. Should be down there by eight o'clock latest.'

'Great. I'll book both you and Bisht into that Mountain View hotel on the outskirts of Haldwani on the Rudrapur road. The farm you have to check out is near Rudrapur. Check into your hotel and then make your plan as you see fit. Keep me in the loop. By the way, our friends from Tinauli are keeping an eye on Gautam and I expect you to be back in his locality in a couple of days anyway.'

'Good,' said Dana. 'I'll let you know when I reach the hotel.'

The Range Rover with local number plates rolled up to the gate of a bungalow on Aurangazeb Lane. They were obviously expected because the gates were promptly opened by a decrepit-looking elderly man and just as promptly shut behind them. The driveway led to a typical Lutyens' Delhi sarkari bungalow—single storeyed and ill maintained. A huge, uncared for lawn in front with barren flowerbeds, scaffolding along one wall and piles of building material scattered about haphazardly added to the picture of neglect and decay.

As the vehicle stopped in the covered porch and Didi

and her companions emerged, Sanju came out of the front door.

'Welcome to my parlour, folks,' he intoned and stopped abruptly. Didi's companions were Jean Pierre and a young woman in a pair of chic and very well-fitting jeans, loose grey tee and Nike running shoes, also grey with a blue swoosh. She was olive skinned, dark haired and wore a headscarf.

Didi smiled. 'This is Farah, and this is our Indian host and controller, Sanjay.'

Sanju recovered quickly and smoothly. '*As-Salaam-alaikum*, Farah.'

'*Wa-alaikum-salaam*,' was the prompt reply from the young lady. 'I am fluent in Arabic, Sanjay, but not in Urdu, unfortunately,' Farah continued in effortless English.

'Use English, that's all you need here,' said Sanju, as he ushered them into the house.

The drawing room was large and in surprisingly good shape with a newly tiled floor, freshly painted walls, comfortable modern furniture and even a couple of prints on the wall—Amrita Sher-Gil and Cezanne. A trolley loaded with glasses, bottles of mineral water and packets of biscuits and chips stood in a corner. Two split AC units kept the room delightfully chilly despite the blazing heat outside.

'Any developments?' asked Sanju, when everyone was seated.

'Nothing yet,' replied Didi. 'Farah and I will, with your permission, be part of the action team for delivering the money and collecting the hostages. You see, our boss considers this mission so important that he withdrew Farah from a sensitive mission at the last minute to join me as backup. Jean Pierre will support us from Delhi. The details of action to be taken will, of course, be worked out when we know exactly how they want to do this exchange. We have acquired local SIM cards, so communications should not be a problem and we have a vehicle with local number plates.'

Sanju nodded approvingly and everyone exchanged numbers.

'We have arranged some telecom equipment in case cellphones are inadequate at any point. Very modern, very small and very French—equipment that we will distribute and demonstrate.' Sanju gestured towards a young man who had entered the room quietly. 'Salim here is part of our... um...action team for this project, assisted by Balwinder—we call him Ballu—who shall be here soon. Ballu will get us some weaponry and a selection of other equipment that we might need.'

'We have small arms we are familiar with, Sanjay, and if you permit, we would like to keep using them. We shall depend on you for heavier stuff if that becomes at all necessary.'

'What calibre?'

'9mm.'

'Ok. Our stuff is the same. Hopefully, we won't need any of it. We have a comm centre here running 24/7 and Salim and Ballu are stationed here too. If we need more people, they are available, even at short notice. Any communication from the kidnappers should be conveyed to us as soon as you get it and we will take it from there. We have two SUVs here and they will be loaded and ready to move as soon as required. The personal equipment, we will distribute to each person as soon as Ballu gets here. And then we go home and wait.'

11

After her conversation with Sanju, Dana was packed and on her way within an hour. Traffic was light, the weather clear and cool, and Dana drove down the hill road at a fast, but controlled pace. She manoeuvred through crowded Raiagar, picked up a little speed and made good time down to Seraghat, where she crossed the Saryu river and began to climb. Driving uphill on a powerful bike enables better control than going downhill and Dana swept up the mountain, reveling in the power of her machine and the sheer beauty of the inner Himalayas. The road was winding, the gradient steep and the mountainside heavily forested. Traffic was light and Dana decided to pushed her bike a little, a bit more than what would be considered safe.

And then an SUV came around a sharp bend, going far too fast for the gradient and barely in control of its mildly inebriated driver. Dana swerved, the driver of the SUV jerked his wheel and skidded and for a second a mishap seemed inevitable. The moment passed, however, as Dana deftly guided her bike away from the road's edge while the Scorpio's tires gained some traction and the vehicle straightened and sped on.

As Dana slowed down to get her mounting anger under control, she realized that she had seen the vehicle before and the driver too was familiar—it was the young tough, the baby of the Ashok gang from Haldwani. They had called him Billu, she remembered. Dana shook her head at the synchronicity and picked up speed—she had no time to waste.

'It's her, Ashok Bhai—it's that bitch from Haldwani!' yelled Billu and stomped on the brakes, nearly precipitating another skid that would have taken them into a deep ravine. 'I swear, it's that fucking cunt. Let's go get her, Ashok Bhai.'

Ashok was also under the influence but lightly.

'You sure? Or is it just tits on a mo-bike that reminds you of her?' he asked.

'Absolutely sure bhai! I recognize the bike, the helmet, the clothes and the tits too, Ashok Bhai! Let's get her, bhai; we may never get another chance!'

Ashok took a quick decision. 'Ok But quickly, Billu, quickly. Just catch up and bump her off the road into the khudd. We have to get to the house near Berinag in time or that bastard Mintu will tell the boss we were late.'

Billu nodded, yanked the Scorpio around and started uphill at high speed.

Dana heard the roar of the pursuing SUV's engine and was tempted to select a suitable place for an ambush and take them out, once and for all. 'Not now,' she told herself and picked up speed. 'Will attract too much attention. Just get on—there's a job to do.'

A slow-moving truck that refused to give way held her back just long enough to enable Billu to catch up and when she overtook the truck and sped up, Billu did likewise, but lost some ground. A couple of overloaded fast-driving taxis came down the hill and Dana's greater manoeuvrability helped her gain a little more distance.

Billu picked up speed only to be restrained by Ashok.

'I said catch up and put her in the khudd, not us, you mad son of a bitch. Slow down a little, she can't get away. And watch your fucking driving.'

Dana picked up speed on a clear stretch and was hoping to drive out of the situation without a confrontation when a mass of stones and mud slid down a section of weak hillside on to the road, inducing a swerve that took the front wheel on to a patch of oil and grease deposited by a generous truck. The resulting skid was uncontrollable and the bike slid towards the edge of the road, smashed through the protective barrier and went over. Dana bailed out just in time, hit the ground rolling and smacked her helmeted head sharply against the blacktopped road. The helmet was of superior quality and prevented any serious injury, but she was in a daze as she came up hard against the metallic remnants of the safety barrier and looked down.

The SUV powered its way uphill and the sound of the engine indicated that it was coming up fast. Dana took a quick though slightly woozy decision, slid over the edge of the road, holding on to it till she was hanging at the full stretch of her arms, then slowly let go. She could only half control her fall and so hurt herself in the process but slid and slithered into the thick oak forest as the Scorpio came to a screeching halt on the road above. The hillside was steep, but not overly so, and Dana positioned herself behind the thick trunk of an ancient oak and took quick stock of herself.

'Nothing broken,' she muttered to herself, a trifle vaguely. 'Just bruises, scrapes and a bump on the head. Nothing you haven't seen before and worse, girl. Keep awake.'

'Congratulations, you bastard,' said Ashok and thumped Billu's back in appreciation as they peered down at the forest that had swallowed the girl and her bike. 'She did it to herself, with just a little bit of help from our Billu! Great, let's get back—that fucker, Mintu, will be calling any minute to check where we are. And remember, the Scorpio was giving some trouble, heating up a little, so we had to stop a while to let it cool down. C'mon, let's go.'

'You don't want to check, Ashok Bhai. She may be injured.'

'You're a mad fucker, Billu. I hope she has broken a few bones and dies down there with a panther or two to get rid of the evidence. C'mon move it now.'

Dana heard the SUV drive off, slowly put away the Glock she had drawn from a zipped pocket of her puffy jacket, put her head down on a heap of oak leaves thinking she would rest for a while.

Time passed and the afternoon slowly drifted towards dusk. Dana awoke with a raging thirst, an aching body and a slightly fuzzy and very painful, head.

'You've been out for a while, babe,' she said to herself and carefully rose up on all fours checking herself for serious hurt and pain and finding nothing very debilitating. She found the bike a few minutes later, untied her duffel and backpack and slowly and painfully climbed up to the road.

Good Samaritans were not lacking for an attractive woman in distress by the roadside and Dana reached Almora in a few hours, checked into the Shikhar Hotel and called Sanju.

'Stay where you are, Dana, see a doctor, rest and get fit. Forget the farmhouse for now. Get some rest, get a local garage to retrieve your bike, and go to your earlier hideout, some village homestay near Gautam's place around Berinag, you said, as soon as you're able, and wait. I'll consult Gautam and get back to you. These guys obviously have a set up in that Seraghat-Raiagar-Berinag area. And Gautam's place is nearby—interesting coincidence.'

Sanju gave a detailed account of the events to Gautam concluding with, 'So what do you think, Buddha, the same gang or two different gangs?'

'It would be one helluva coincidence, Sanju, if two different gangs this well-organized are both located in the same area—or, at least, have a hideout here. There's every likelihood of it being one gang with multiple big operations; which makes them all the more dangerous. This Pandit character appeared quite capable of running big ops and he did say something about having some important business to take care of when he allowed me ten days to pack up and get out of here.'

'Time will tell, G. Anyway, for now we'll just go with the flow. When instructions for dropping off the money come through, we might have a clearer picture. I have a separate team for the French problem and Dana will be stationed near your place to check out this Ashok bastard and his team and help you with this Pandit character as required. You have Dana's number and she will call as soon as she reaches her village safe house. And if it's all this Pandit's doing, wonderful—we'll just take him out and solve both issues at one stroke.'

Gautam laughed softly. 'Always the eternal optimist, eh, Sanju. But if you need Dana, don't hesitate to take her away. I went over to Tinauli after Pandit's visit and discussed strategy with them. The youngsters will be coming over a couple days before the deadline he's given me and we'll sort this business out. You keep your focus on your official matter. Anyway, we'll keep in touch and coordinate.'

'Sure thing, G. The great coordinator, that's me! But remember, Dana is there for you to use as required. Take care, bye.'

12

Mintu Mobile was slumped in a battered old armchair on the porch of the dilapidated house, smoking one of the forty odd cigarettes he consumed a day, when Ashok and Billu drove up.

'Where the fuck have you been, you bastards? He's already called once to check up and he's sounding seriously pissed.'

Mintu never raised his voice above a deep and not unpleasant growl that seemed to emerge from way within his humongous, hairy chest.

'Vehicle was giving trouble—had to stop and fix it. What bee has got up your arse, Mintu? What's the problem?' replied Ashok

'The problem, you cunt, is that he wants me for something immediately—something urgent—and because of you I'll have to drive half the fucking night to get there.'

'Hey, hey and fuck you too, Mintu. What does that have to do with me? I lost just forty-five minutes or so and I've been driving through for almost five hours without even a piss break.'

Mintu stubbed out the cigarette he had been smoking.

'Oye, Pintu—they are here. Load up the gaadi while I brief them. We leave in five minutes.'

Mintu was Pandit's senior-most team leader, the most seasoned criminal with four murders behind him and an enormous capacity for violence that even Ashok was wary of.

'There's a foreign couple in the inner bedroom. They are not allowed outside the room, except for an hour in the morning and an hour in the evening under guard, understand? They are not to be harmed in any way—kept in perfect condition, ok? The chowkidar cooks for them and knows the routine. Just keep them here until you get different orders from himself. Think you can do that without written instructions?'

'Screw you, Mintu. I'll manage,' replied Ashok. 'Billu bring the bags in and get some tea and food organized. And be nice to the old man in the kitchen; he's a rough old bastard by all accounts?'

'Yes, but he can cook a good meal if you keep him happy,' observed Mintu as he heaved his bulk out of the chair and moved to his SUV parked in front of the house. 'Remember, they are needed in perfect condition, Ashok. Be careful.'

Mintu's two team members emerged from the house, loaded the vehicle and drove away without any further conversation.

13

Ruth Friedman, Principal Security Officer at the Israeli Embassy in New Delhi, landed early morning at the Indira Gandhi International Airport and took a cab to her flat near the Embassy complex on APJ Abdul Kalam Marg. At nine o'clock, she walked across to the Embassy and into her boss's room to report arrival.

'You're looking very fit, Ruth,' observed Brigadier Ari Dayan, Head of Intelligence and Security at the Israeli Embassy, as he gestured her to a chair. 'Worked you hard, did they, in the desert?'

Ruth nodded. 'As hard as you used to, boss. They needed to reassure themselves that I had recovered completely, so they kept pushing, the bastards.'

'If you insist on getting shot in the line of duty in faraway India what do you expect the Head Office boys to do, Ruth. They have to ensure you are fighting fit. Hope you didn't lose your famous temper and put someone in hospital.'

Ruth laughed. 'Almost, boss, almost. But I'm older and a little wiser, so I restrained myself. But it was a close thing. How have things been here? Quiet, I'm told.'

The Brigadier nodded. 'Yes, for the most part. The French are in a bit of a tizzy. Their President's best friend's daughter has been kidnapped with her boyfriend in the Kumaon and they've sent in a team to coordinate recovery ops with the Indians. Your friend, Mr Datta, is running things from the domestic end, I understand.'

'And we are interested in this, why?' asked Ruth.

'I got a call from our American friends. Apparently, the French asked them and they in turn thought it fit to consult me in the matter. They are well aware of our newly developing relationship, of course. I told them Datta was the right person for this problem and that is it. You approve, Major?'

Ruth grinned. 'Oh absolutely, sir. And my approval matters a great deal to you, of course!'

Brig. Dayan smiled back. 'It matters a great deal, Major. They asked me about your friend, the Colonel, too; very curious they were, insistent, in fact, for an update on his "status" shall we say?'

Ruth's expression hardened a trifle. 'And you told them what?'

'Oh, simply the truth, Ruth. That I had never met the gentleman, and to the best of my knowledge, he was living a retired life somewhere wild and remote. Besides, I understood that their DEA people had worked with him closely on some matter, so they probably knew more than I did about him.'

'They are real bastards, aren't they? Anyway, since things are quiet and a long weekend is coming up, I plan to go visit my Colonel, with your permission, Brigadier. Will be back Monday night.'

'Sure, carry on. Your assistant has actually learnt to take responsibility in your absence. A long weekend on duty will be his reward. Give my best to the Colonel.'

'Thank you, sir, I will,' replied Ruth and left the room.

Pandit briefed Mintu in detail about the plan for exchanging the ransom for the hostages and sent him on his way.

'Stay at the farm till I give you the word and no wandering about, Mintu. Keep your heads down and live quietly till this job's over. Then you can all take the bonus and enjoy a good holiday, which, I'm sure, you'll earn.'

Mintu left with his boys and Pandit summoned Pradeep Shah, one of his senior team leaders from Nainital.

'We need another murga, Pradeep,' said Pandit. 'This is turning out to be a good line of business.'

'Foreign and rich, eh boss?' asked Pradeep, a short but very tough thug—the ne'er-do-well younger son of a well-to-do hotelier family of Nainital.

'Yes, that combination seems to work well for us. So, go and find us another target. Look for fancy cars, self-driven. Use your judgment. I'll monitor Mintu and the exchange, and I have some other business to attend to near Jhaltola. Keep me in the loop—report every evening as always.'

'Sure, boss,' said Pradeep and left with his two associates.

14

Ruth went shopping in Khan Market the day before her departure for the hills. Gautam lived a rather spartan life in his mountain refuge, so Ruth shopped for goodies not easily available in the Kumaon. She stocked up with good wine and cheese, olive oil and olives, crackers for the cheese and other indulgences. Her personal stuff went into her backpack, the shopping into a duffle and very early morning, just pre-dawn, she fired up her Jeep Wrangler and set off towards the mountains. As she often did on long drives, Ruth chatted with her Wrangler as she drove out of a slumbering Delhi and on to the highway that led via Garhmukteshwar, to the Kumaon.

'Good to be going to the hills, eh baby?' she asked the softly growling Jeep. 'Wonder what he's been doing in my absence apart from experimenting with potatoes. The wheat harvest was good he said in his last mail, and the fruit trees are coming on well. The herb garden that Annie planted has taken hold and he doesn't know what to do with all the exotica it is yielding. I'll take a whole lot back to Delhi—they are so damned expensive here.'

Ruth crossed the Ganges at Garh in very good time, but then was stuck short of Moradabad for several hours; a fully loaded truck had overturned and crashed into a tractor trolley and traffic was backed up for more than a kilometre. Enterprising drivers had jumped the divider and gone on to the wrong side of the road creating a logjam on that side too, accompanied by much shouting, yelling and demonstrations of aggression. Ruth had a full tank of gas, an excellent functioning AC and a large selection of music on her phone; she suffered the delay with much of her composure intact. Once clear of the jam she took the Bazpur-Kaladhungi road which was mostly empty of traffic, and reached Singh Sweets by one o'clock. She exchanged formal greetings with old Singh Sahib, who was, as always, at the till by eleven every morning, had a hot and heavy lunch and drove up into the mountains with a sigh of relief.

'I know he grows veggies, but not everything, right?' she muttered as she breezed up the old Bhowali road via the Sanatorium, her mood lifting as the air cooled. It was a weekday and traffic was light. 'And he hasn't got any fruit yet, so let's pick up some at Bhowali.'

Everybody, especially tourists, stopped at Bhowali to buy fruit, so Pradeep hired a room in the hotel just beyond the bridge, parked his vehicle in front, off the road, and settled down to check out the tourist traffic. One of his boys was always in the SUV while one slept, and Pradeep wandered around the market at odd hours of the day and night on the lookout for potential targets.

'What is that nasty bastard, Pradeep, doing hanging around Bhowali? It's been three days now and the fucker's still here,' asked a fruit seller to the restaurant owner, whose establishment had the dubious distinction of having Pradeep as customer.

Ravi, the restaurateur to whom the question was addressed, looked up from the omelette cooking slowly for a Delhi party, who had stopped for a meal.

'Why don't you ask him yourself, you silly bugger? Just don't come to me later to have your arse stitched up, that's all!'

'Oi, take it easy, bastard. Just a random thought, that's all,' protested the curious vendor. 'Don't get all excited.'

Ravi shook his head in exasperation. 'You never had any brains did you, arsehole. You don't have random thoughts about Pradeep—not if you want to keep your family jewels in working condition! Now fuck off and sell some rotten peaches to some fucking tourists who don't know any better. I've got work to do.'

As the fruit seller returned to his cart, a Jeep Wrangler in prime condition drove up and stopped by his cart. Despite Ravi's critical observation, the vendor had very good quality fruit and the attractive foreigner who got out of the SUV soon bought several of his offerings and then wandered off in search of fresh vegetables.

The afternoon was sliding slowly towards dusk and Pradeep was thinking of tea when he saw the Jeep and its single, female, foreign occupant alight in search of fruit and veg.

'Thank you, God,' he muttered as he shook his dozing companion awake. 'I was going out of my mind. Here, Sunny, go wake up that bastard, Harish, and get him here. Five minutes, no more. Quickly now, go.'

Pradeep's boys knew better than to delay when their boss used that particular tone of voice. Sunny muttered a feeble protest and hurried off to get his partner from the hotel, while Pradeep started the vehicle and turned it around ready to follow his selected target down the hill. There was no hurry, Pradeep knew. There was too much traffic on the road—a national highway—at that time. They would follow the target, see where she was going and make a plan as matters became clearer. But the opportunity was heaven sent.

As Ruth drove down the hill from Bhowali to Garampani, she noted that a dusty, but not old, SUV was trailing her and despite her very moderate pace had not overtaken her in over half an hour. Hill drivers are not bashful about getting ahead of anything in front of them and she was a little curious about this evidence of restraint on Uttarakhand roads by local lads. She had noted the UK registration when she had passed the stationary vehicle just after the Bhowali bridge.

'Maybe he's just hungover,' she said to herself thoughtfully, although that had never stopped any red-blooded Pahari boy from racing downhill, overtaking everything in his path as a matter of izzat.

'You are paranoid by nature and by training,' she muttered to herself, but nonetheless pulled over by the side of the road after crossing Garampani village. She got out, stretched and stood casually admiring the view of the Kosi river, looking downstream towards Garampani. Ruth pulled out her cellphone, took several photographs of the river and soon enough the SUV she was waiting for came zipping along at a fast clip and she shot a long video that happened to include a usable picture of the license plate and a blurred one of the three men in the vehicle.

Five minutes later Ruth started up and drove on.

'If they are actually trailing me for some strange reason, they will wait just before the bridge, after which the climb up to Almora begins,' she said to herself. 'There's a new road that takes off towards Mukteshwar from there and they would need to keep track of where I'm going, right?'

Ruth laughed at herself and sped up. She was a long way from home still.

The SUV was, in fact, parked a little short of the bridge, the three men smoking and chatting casually, as Ruth passed them.

'It's still not conclusive evidence,' said Ruth to herself, but notched up the alertness level a little.

15

Dana had checked into the Shikhar Hotel on reaching Almora and asked the hotel management for a good doctor. She'd got her cuts and bruises attended to, taken a Tetanus Toxide shot and dutifully swallowed the antibiotics and painkillers the doctor prescribed. The doctor also prescribed rest for mild concussion and Dana obeyed, reluctantly. Her bike was salvaged for a princely sum and returning late evening after inspecting it and approving expensive repairs, she saw, to her utter surprise, Ruth driving in through the hotel gates.

Dana and Ruth had been members of a special ops unit of the Israel Defence Forces for a time—nobody lasted very long in such units—and had participated in some rather nasty strikes deep in Lebanon before being shifted to less demanding assignments.

Dana had come to India as part of an Israeli training team for an Indian paramilitary force—part of a defense cooperation agreement—and stayed on when the assignment finished. Planning for a quiet life by the sea for the foreseeable future, she had settled in a remote south Goa location close to a small fishing village that boasted of a tiny church, a general merchants shop and a handful of houses scattered amidst palm trees close to the shoreline.

Ruth had stayed on in the IDF, first in hospital and rehab centres recovering from battlefield injuries, and then in a series of Headquarter postings till an old boss had asked for her by name for a diplomatic post in New Delhi. Brigadier Dayan had led the unit in which both Dana and Ruth had served, fought and suffered grievous injury. When he had been given the post in India, he had asked for Ruth to be his Security Officer; he felt she needed a change after the rather stressful years spent in frontline operations, and the Brigadier knew well that Post Traumatic Stress Syndrome took many forms.

The New Delhi posting was a fairly relaxed one and Ruth gradually lost the fine-drawn, rather brittle appearance she presented to the world. As the knots within eased, the inevitable happened. A chance meeting with Gautam at a party in Datta's house kindled a spark that blossomed rather quickly into a relationship, which promised a depth that both parties were strangers to. Given their circumstances, the future was hard to decipher but what was present was enormously powerful.

Effusive greetings were not quite their style, so after a quick, brief hug Ruth said, 'I'm bursting. I need a pee. Grab a table in the café, Dana, and we'll have coffee and you'll tell me what the hell you're up to here.'

Dana, a person of few words, smiled briefly, nodded, and the two entered the hotel lobby together.

'I was on a holiday—trekking in the Munsiyari region—when Sanju called about Colonel Shukla's problem,' said Dana, when Ruth emerged from the Ladies and sat down at the table.

Ruth sat up straight. 'What problem is the Colonel facing? I thought he'd just got back from Japan. I got back a couple of days ago and decided to give him a surprise. I haven't talked to anyone in the Datta gang.'

'Some local goons are threatening the Colonel, asking him to sell his property or else,' explained Dana. 'When he got back from Japan he found these guys had gone to his place and left a message with his manager, Joshiji. Broken two of his fingers to underline the message, too.'

'Fuck! And what has Gautam done about it?'

'He's apparently said he will do as they say and asked for time to pack up. He's also told Sanju that he will deal with it and they need not deploy any resources for this. I was in the region, so Sanju asked me to hang around, just in case.'

Ruth shook her head impatiently. 'He's just buying time to finalize strategy. Those guys don't know what's coming their way, the bastards.'

'I agree. I'm going to stay an hour's drive from his place in a village homestay. What are you planning?'

'To go up and help, of course. But what are you doing in this place instead of your village whatever?'

Dana then briefed her on the kidnapping of the French couple and Datta and Sanju's involvement in it.

'Yeah, I heard about the French case in office. Everyone's covering their ass, as always.'

Ruth paused, thought for a moment, then told Dana about her suspicion about being followed from Bhowali. 'If these guys are looking for easy targets for ransom, foreigners—especially women—in fancy cars would be the right choice, no?'

Dana nodded. 'If that is, in fact, the case, what do you

want to do? We can just go on to the Colonel's place as planned and if anyone tries messing around, we just take them out and dump them in a quiet spot. Plenty of those around here.'

Ruth nodded thoughtfully. 'Or we go along and dismantle their whole set up. Might be some dividends in that.'

Dana shook her head and laughed. 'And I was considered the reckless one! Remember what that bastard Abramovitz used to say?'

Ruth smiled and said in deep voiced, heavily accented Hebrew, 'You are young and tough and very well trained, but you are not superhuman. Those who think they are, underestimate the enemy and die first!'

'Melodramatic, but true, Ruth. Too many unknowns there.'

Ruth countered with a question. 'What are you carrying?'

'A Glock, for which Sanju has got me an all India license, a knife in my boot and one spare. Four loaded mags.'

'Good. I'm carrying my Beretta and my old Gerber. So, we are well equipped, right?'

'That's not the point, Ruth. We can probably manage without any equipment, unless there are too many of them. But do you want to do it this way? It is complicated and uncertain. Let us simply go to the Colonel and support whatever he is planning to do.'

'Look, if there is actually an attempt to hijack us, then it has to be the same gang, right? And they may well be the guys targeting Gautam too—there can't be two such gangs in this small region. This is supposed to be a crime-free countryside, for God's sake! So if we are attacked and the objective is kidnapping for ransom, we go along and sort them out—many birds and one stone!'

Dana grinned. 'Your motives are quite clear, Ruth. But if they try to get rough, then?'

Ruth grinned back. 'Then I rely on my fearsome warrior comrade to assist me in putting them down and walking away, what else? You don't have to, Dana, but decide quickly, please. It's getting late and we have a good three hours' drive ahead of us.'

Dana shrugged. 'I have no wish to drive in a local taxi for three hours in the dark. Besides, let's give them the darkness—might encourage them to make their move. You know I like the dark. What cover stories?'

'Are you carrying your passport? I'm carrying a certified copy,' said Ruth.

'Same here. Hide them and pretend to be Americans?'

'Great! You're the Yank with a rich father and I'm your friend with no family anymore, but some inherited money.'

'But how long can we sustain that? They will ask for parents' contact numbers, emails, addresses and so forth and we'll be exposed.'

'Come on, Dana! I'm just looking to identify the gang and their hideout if possible, not spend any great length of time there! The moment we've got as much as possible or are in danger of exposure, we take them out and leave. Just a quick information gathering op, in and out.'

Dana shook her head doubtfully. 'The Colonel will kill me if you get hurt, dearie!'

Ruth laughed. 'Never thought I'd see the great Dana preaching caution! But the choice is yours. Make up your mind and let's move.'

Dana nodded acquiescence and Ruth got up.

'Good. Let's eat something and set out soon and see what happens.'

~

They left as the shadows were lengthening and found the dusty SUV waiting a little beyond the Shikhar Hotel. It was behind them as they turned up the hill to get to the Pithoragarh road and was behind them as they passed Chitai.

'You are probably right about these guys targeting us. But it's still not established,' commented Dana, as they started climbing up from the valley bottom to Barechhina.

'We'll fill up at the petrol pump at 'Chhina and once we turn off towards Seraghat and Berinag we have to look out for any move they might make. The road has much less traffic, especially at night.'

'I can think of some likely spots, if they are quick and efficient,' replied Dana.

'And if they search us properly, they will find the weapons. We'll have to do an immediate breakout then and that will be risky,' said Ruth thoughtfully.

'Unlikely,' replied Dana. 'Women are not seen as bearers of weapons; the context is wrong. We are helpless targets, remember.'

'We'd better act like that, Dana. Don't go into aggression mode, please.'

Dana laughed. 'Yes, Captain, oh sorry, Major, I mean. You know I always obey orders.'

'Of course, you do. Who better to vouch for that than me, right?'

Dana grinned and said nothing.

16

'There's no traffic behind us for at least a couple of kilometres. Harish, you get off at that bridge that is being repaired and roll a couple of boulders on to the road. That will stop any other traffic coming up on us. Then start walking down. We'll overtake them and pick them up very quickly. Good, she's picked up a friend—adds to the money! I'll go with them in their vehicle and Sunny will come back and pick you up. We'll go to the second cottage down the road from Raiagar, not the one where those Frenchies are—not enough room. Is it clear?'

Both Sunny and Harish acknowledged the instructions. Like all Pradeep's operations, it was clearly thought out and relied on speed and efficiency for successful execution. There was also an element of risk, always. The boys suspected it was the adrenaline rush that their boss relished most; that and the money, of course. Pandit, though ruthlessly demanding, paid well for work well done.

'They have sped up. Catching up fast,' said Dana, who was watching their back trail.

'Ok. There's no traffic—probably planning a quick snatch and grab. Shows initiative.'

They slowed down to walking speed to cross a bridge under repair. A retaining wall was being built and only a narrow uneven strip of unpaved track was available for traffic. Headlights behind them grew brighter.

They bumped across and Ruth gunned the Jeep.

'Let's see what they are made of, Dana,' said Ruth as she accelerated away.

'Careful, we don't want to lose them,' warned Dana.

Ruth grinned and slowed down. 'You're a spoilsport, but you're right. Not here for the fun of racing down the hill in my little beauty. We have work to do.'

Ruth slowed and soon a bright pair of headlights was flickering at them asking for way.

Ruth saw a suitable spot, moved over, slowed down and flicked on her right-turn indicator—a Pahari indication by a leading vehicle to one following to overtake it.

The SUV overtook the Jeep then screeched to a halt blocking the road. The front passenger side door opened and Pradeep came out very quickly, gun in hand, and ran up to the driver's side of the Jeep. He thrust the gun through the open window till it touched Ruth's forehead.

'Don't move, you, driver!' he shouted, his tone loud, confident and commanding. 'Or you are dead. Open the back door, quick.'

Ruth looked frightened and immediately complied. He got in, seated himself and tapped the back of Ruth's head with the gun barrel. 'Now just do as you are told and you will not be hurt. Understand?'

Ruth said in shaky tones, 'Yes, yes, but please, what do you want? What is going on here?'

As soon as Pradeep had climbed into Ruth's Jeep, the SUV, which had reversed in the meantime, sped away back up the hill.

'Now just drive carefully and you'll be all right. You will not be harmed if you simply do as you're told. Is that clear?'

Both Ruth and Dana noted the excellent command over English that their abductor displayed and his educated, cultured diction.

'Give me your cellphones, please, and do not try any communication with anyone in any way, ok? Cellphones, please. All of them. Don't let me find any on you or in your luggage later.'

Dana and Ruth wordlessly handed over their mobile phones.

'Good, now don't worry and don't do anything foolish. As I said, you will not be harmed if you simply obey orders. You will have a nice holiday in a mountain cottage with a phenomenal view of the Himalayas and then you will go home as soon as your family gives us what we want, which is just some money. Ok? A business transaction, nothing more. Just relax, take it easy and don't panic and do anything that will get you hurt. Now, just follow the road till I tell you different. It's a bit of a drive.'

Five minutes later, Dana spoke up in a shaky, tearful voice.

'Please, we are just tourists in your beautiful country, please don't hurt us. We'll do anything you say, but please don't hurt us.'

Pradeep said in a quiet reassuring tone, 'I've already told you, nobody will harm you as long as you do as you are told. Now relax and let your friend concentrate on driving. Hill driving is tricky at night.'

'Are you ladies familiar with this area?' asked Pradeep casually, after a long period of silence. 'Been here before, on a previous visit, perhaps?'

'Oh no, never seen the Kumaon hills before,' replied Dana. 'We were planning to find a resort with a good view of the Himalayas—there are many in the area, I believe.'

'No reservations, then?' queried Pradeep. 'This is high season, you know.'

'True, but we checked availability online and rooms are available in all the resorts near Berinag. We don't like to plan over much. A bit of uncertainty is quite fun and if need be, we can always sleep in this vehicle.'

'Well, I can promise you a mountain view better than any resort, but our facilities are a trifle basic; very clean, though, and the cook's quite good. You won't have any problem, I assure you,' replied Pradeep and lapsed into silence.

They drove on, and an hour after Raiagar, Pradeep guided them on to a track going up the mountainside. It was narrow, but just about adequate for the Wrangler and after half an hour of careful driving, the pine trees gave way to oak. Fifteen minutes into the oak forest, the track ended in a large clearing that boasted of a good-sized traditional hill cottage—two storeyed, stone walls, patal roof. A small, but vigorous little rivulet flowed through one corner of the property and filled a concrete water storage tank on its way down the hill. A huge Bhutia dog with a shaggy golden coat and a deep aggressive bark ran up as they stopped before the cottage. A tall light pole with a solar-powered bulb lit up the area and an old man, who was obviously the caretaker of the place, stood under it.

'Careful now, ladies,' cautioned Pradeep. 'This one is not very friendly. Let Pandeji tie him up and then you can get down.'

Pradeep's henchmen in their SUV were close behind them and both Dana and Ruth noted that no vehicle doors were opened until the dog was safely secured.

'Here you are, ladies,' announced Pradeep, as he

ushered them into a smallish room equipped with two beds, a battered old wooden armchair and an old but serviceable wooden table holding a jug of water and two glasses. The one window had iron bars across it and a faded curtain for privacy. A narrow door led to a bathroom that was small but clean and equipped with a western style WC and a small washbasin.

'See, all the comforts of home!' announced Pradeep, jovially. 'The menu is limited—we are really in the wilds here—but quite adequate, and tea and coffee are available on demand. The water in that jug is pure Himalayan spring water that you would pay ten dollars a pop for in a five-star hotel in Delhi. Settle down, relax and we will chat in the morning. Dinner will be served in a short while.'

'No need for immediate action, apparently,' commented Ruth in Hebrew when Pradeep and his gang had left, and lay down on one of the beds.

'Doesn't look like it,' replied Dana, also in Hebrew. She moved around apparently restless and ill at ease.

'No cameras, I think,' she said after a while and Ruth assented.

Dana then set about looking for concealed microphones and after twenty careful minutes sat down and nodded an all clear.

'Four-hour watches. You get some sleep after they give us dinner; you've been driving,' said Dana and Ruth nodded.

Dana stretched and lay down on the empty bed. 'So how are things back home? We don't get much coverage of Israeli affairs here.'

'Same old, same old. The more things change, the more they remain the same, unfortunately. We will be at war—covert and overt—forever as far as I can see.'

'Certainly looks like it. Which is why I opted out—I could no longer see the point of it.'

'But you couldn't handle the peace either eh? The cottage by the sea in a little fishing village, how long did that last?'

Dana laughed. 'I still have my cottage and spend a fair amount of time there! But yes, I couldn't manage the quiet country existence for very long. I did try, very hard though but in the end fate intervened and brought me back into active life.'

'Fate, was it?' said Ruth with a smile. 'Do tell, what happened to get you active again?'

Dana got up and stood by the window, staring at a huge old oak tree with unseeing eyes.

'It was a beautiful winter day, like so many before it, and I was bored out of my mind. I decided to go for a long drive to the North where a young couple from my village—yes, I see it as my village—had recently opened a small beach shack—Goan food and beer by the sea—beautiful. The drive was fun, dodging fast-moving taxis, pigs, two-wheelers and strollers on Goa's narrow roads. The lunch was great too, until two drunk buffoons came along and ruined the party.'

Ruth shook her head in mild disbelief. 'I don't believe this, two drunks was what it took to push you into action again!'

'The drunks were nothing—just punks who thought they were tough enough to terrorize small businessmen and molest young women and get away with it. I showed them the error of their ways and they apologized and went away very soon. The problem was two serious middle-aged men were having lunch at the shack at that time. I saw them when I came in and ignored them—they weren't creating any trouble. But two days later I got a message—through the young couple who ran the shack—that they wanted to meet for a business discussion. I had nothing better to do so I met them. And that is where it all started.'

'"It" being your becoming an enforcer for a local gang?'

Dana grinned. 'Don't try and provoke me, Ruthie! Just ask and I shall tell. I remained a freelance specialist—started with a couple of escort jobs when they were moving sensitive consignments across state lines and then a few underworld hits. I had made it clear that I would select jobs on a case-to-case basis; and was careful to choose only criminal targets. No police force worries too much when hoods get killed—saves them the effort of doing it themselves. Anyway, I was selective and very very careful until an error of judgement brought your worthy Colonel, Sanju and you into my orbit and offered me an alternative to follow. And here we are!'

Ruth laughed out loud. 'Neatly put Dana! But euphemisms apart, it's better to be a government gun, however informal, than a private hitter—wouldn't you agree!'

But by now Dana had had enough confessional conversation. 'I'm hungry—trust they intend to feed us properly.'

Shortly thereafter, a simple but satisfactory meal was served. With dinner done, Ruth slept and Dana kept first watch.

The night passed uneventfully.

Tea—hot, sweet and strong—was served at seven and a breakfast of egg bhurji and parathas at eight. Pradeep appeared after the breakfast things were cleared away.

'A lovely morning, ladies. Would you like to stretch your legs a little before we get down to business? Just remember, you can't run and you can't hide. We know every inch of these woods and there's the dog, too. So come along outside and admire the snow view before the haze covers it. We'll talk when we get back.'

The view of the Himalayas was indeed magnificent; not quite 180 degrees, but close enough. A reasonably short walk along a narrow footpath and there they were—the eternal snows gleaming in the morning sun. They stood and watched in silence and then the haze began to build up and they started back.

'Tomorrow you should come up here at sunrise. The mountains slowly turn from grey to pink; it's quite a sight ladies, believe me,' said Pradeep, as they walked down the hill. He evidently was proud of his land and his hotelier family's genes, though he had deviated into quite a different line of work.

'And now to business, please,' he said, as they sat down on folding chairs in front of the house. 'Tell me your names and details of who to contact for your ransom. And please don't be clever and try to hide things. We are reasonable people and one million dollars per head is all we want. No more and certainly no less. Any problems with that?'

Ruth shook her head slowly. 'Look, we are not poor, we are well qualified and have good jobs, but we don't have that kind of money. We can't raise that kind of money, no way.'

Pradeep's voice hardened. 'Don't bullshit me, lady. It won't work. You have families, don't you? They can help and they must. Believe me you don't want to spend the rest of your life chained to the bedpost in a crib catering to truck drivers. That will be your fate if you can't raise the money. We'll simply sell you off to the highest bidder—and young white women fetch a good price! Think about it. I'll be back in a while. Work it out and let me know. I don't have time to waste.'

Pradeep strode into the house and slammed the front door behind him.

'He's bluffing, I suspect,' said Dana. 'He'll be in trouble if he has selected targets who cannot be ransomed.'

'I agree, but let's not waste time. Let's be suitably terrified and reveal that our families can possibly raise the money if we convince them of the horrors that await us if they don't.'

'Ok. Let's get this over with,' responded Dana.

Pradeep returned in half an hour.

'So, what have you decided?' he asked harshly. 'Your fate in your hands, ladies. Speak and quickly.'

Ruth spoke, hesitantly, timidly; obviously frightened.

'Look, we want to get back home unharmed. So we will speak to our families and persuade them to help us out. They love us and will do the needful, I'm sure. It might take them a little time, but they will raise the money. Just let us get in touch with them, please.'

'Good. See how simple it is,' beamed Pradeep. 'Now for the details, please. Here are pens and paper; please write down all the information we need—names, addresses, phone numbers, email ids, ranks/positions of parents, profession, blah blah blah. Once I've studied the data, we'll have a chat to clarify any doubts I have and then, while we arrange things, you relax and enjoy a short Himalayan holiday in the lap of nature far from the madding crowd, eh?'

17

In Tinauli village, Deborah summoned Yaakov and Ben after lunch, served them coffee and sat them down on her porch.

'Ok, boys, where are we on this Colonel Shukla matter?' she asked.

'The bikes are serviced and kept at a friend's house one village down the road from the Colonel's,' reported Yaakov. 'It's now two days from the deadline given by this Pandit character, so we thought we'd sneak into the Colonel's place late tonight and plan for D-Day. That's day after. See what he has in mind and position ourselves accordingly.'

Deborah nodded agreement. 'Yes. He said he needed you for reconnaissance, so you'll have to be stationed appropriately. But what did you get on this Pandit fellow? Anything more than what we already know?'

'A little,' replied Ben. 'He has some sort of base around the Berinag-Raiagar area. That's not far from the Colonel's place. He's also a very rough customer personally and has a bunch of tough guys in teams of three or four, all of whom are genuinely scared of him. But he pays well and is smart—not to be underestimated.'

'So, he'll have someone watching the Colonel's place for sure,' commented Deborah.

'The road to the Colonel's place takes off from the main road, about two kilometres from the village. He'll probably have someone in the village looking out for unusual traffic,' Ben remarked.

'That's a little iffy,' objected Deborah. 'He may well have posted people on the ridge overlooking the estate and someone on the road leading up the hill to the house. Do not underrate the opposition boys.'

Yaakov nodded. 'Sure, but they won't be hanging around the forests too much in advance—not practical. That's why we'll reach there tonight, get in position tomorrow daytime, and sit quietly, waiting for any unwanted visitors.'

'Ok. Off you go then. And report regularly if you can get through. Good thing it's full moon tonight and not a cloud in the sky.'

The day before the deadline given to Gautam, Pandit moved to the cottage where the French couple were housed. As the afternoon advanced, he grew increasingly troubled and uneasy—something he was unused to in the normal course. The quiet Colonel bothered him. He had been prepared for loud words, aggressive exchanges and postures, all of which he was very good at dealing with. But the fellow had just thought for a while and then crumbled without any face-saving belligerence at all! And that, after he had first stood in front of the speeding vehicle coming straight at him without turning a hair. The complete absence of bluster and bravado from a man being dispossessed of his retirement home, which was also a prime piece of property, was unusual and troubling.

Coming to a decision, Pandit went to the door of the cottage and yelled for Ram Singh, his favourite troubleshooter, who had been summoned from his village and was awaiting orders. When the wiry ex subedar-major appeared, Pandit sat him down and spoke to him at length. Pandit's instructions were always clear and detailed and repeated several times. No one could later argue that he had misunderstood—not that anybody had the gumption to mess up things and then argue with Pandit.

Ram Singh packed his rucksack, had an early dinner, and commandeered a vehicle and driver from Pradeep.

'Wake me up at twelve and drop me off beyond the Colonel Sahib's village by three, Sunny. I want to be in position before dawn,' instructed Ram Singh. He slept for five hours and then left as planned.

~

Gautam had an early supper, read for a while, then set the alarm for 3 a.m. and went to sleep. By three-thirty, he was at a preselected vantage point on the ridge above his estate, warmly clad in black track pants, black t-shirt and a black fleece jacket. His trekking shoes were also black, as was the backpack he carried. As the sky lightened and dawn slowly approached, he began scanning the ridge carefully with his combat grade binoculars. He did a wide sweep of the forest below him, starting at the farthest point that his device permitted and slowly coming in closer. He found nothing untoward in his first sweep, but it was still quite dark and the full moon created a lot of shadowy patches in the heavily wooded mountainside. With this in mind,

Gautam began a slow second sweep, this time starting close and moving out.

~

The Israelis had moved into position the previous afternoon. Ben stayed below Gautam's estate, off the approach road leading up to the gate, while Yaakov climbed up to a high point on the ridge overlooking the property. Despite knowing that Gautam would be up on the ridge early morning for a look around, Yaakov did not hear or spot him.

~

Ram Singh was the last to arrive—climbing up from the road to the ridge overlooking Gautam's estate took time and effort; it had to be done by moonlight and silently. He was very good in the woods—he had been an instructor in the mountain warfare school of the Indian Army before he was sacked for certain serious discrepancies in the records of the ammunition and small arms store of which he was in charge. Age and a weakness for strong drink, aggravated by his unceremonious exit, had impacted his stamina a little, but all other skills remained intact. Ram Singh got dropped off on the motor road after passing the Colonel's estate and climbed up to find a suitable spot on the high ground above the target area.

Sound carries very far in the still and silent Himalayan nights. Ram Singh's arrival was thus announced softly but clearly to everyone keeping vigil on the mountainside, by the sound of the diesel SUV that conveyed him to the vicinity of Gautam's place.

Thereafter, however, his expertise stood him in good stead. Ram Singh made his way up the hill very slowly and silently and settled down in a spot that had a clear view of the house below. The driveway, the front porch and the main entrance to the bungalow were visible without any obstruction. He settled down to wait with a sigh of satisfaction. It was too early to unpack his equipment. He would do that when the sun was up. He had plenty of time—Pandit would not be there for several hours yet.

When dawn was imminent, Ben decided to move. He was sure that whoever had come to the area in the vehicle in the early hours had not come to his zone of responsibility, but had chosen to go up to the ridge above the house. Yaakov would look after matters there, so Ben moved down to the kuchha track, walked up to the gate, which was unlocked and let himself in. Joshiji's light came on and he peered out of the door to be greeted in fluent Pahari by the young Israeli, who then continued up to the house.

Yaakov waited motionless for the light to strengthen and for whoever had come up from the road to reveal himself—a deep breath, a dislodged stone, a fart, a rustle of clothing against a tree trunk, anything at all. But nothing happened until a small stone hit his back lightly. He turned quickly to find Gautam ten feet behind him, finger on his lips. Yaakov nodded in acknowledgement and slowly moved up to the Colonel. Gautam moved carefully up the ridge and along it for a while, then stopped and reached for his binoculars. Yaakov did the same and the two began to search the area below them very, very slowly and carefully.

Yaakov's young eyes spotted the anomaly first and when he gestured and Gautam focused his attention on the area indicated, Ram Singh decided to move. It was light enough to assemble his equipment and he pulled his rucksack closer, opened it and took out the disassembled components of a modern sniper rifle complete with an infrared telescopic sight and began to put the weapon together. The movements were sufficient for the two watchers to locate the hidden man and identify exactly what he was doing.

Gautam took out his muted cellphone and began typing a set of instructions for Yaakov, who read and acknowledged them. Gautam patted his shoulder and moved away quietly.

Once he was beyond eyeshot and earshot of the hidden sniper, he moved quickly along the ridge descending only when the ridge curved and brought him to a spot behind the house that was not easily visible from Ram Singh's location.

He entered the house through the same door he had exited by, the kitchen door at the back, and found Ben brewing tea and chatting with the dogs at his feet.

'Morning, Colonel. I was going to sit outside the kitchen door, out of sight of the fellow who came up in the early hours, till someone woke up, but I found it open and guessed you had gone out on recee, sir,' said Ben. 'Did you get the guy who came visiting? Tea will be ready in a minute.'

Gautam nodded briefly. 'Will you bring it to the drawing room, Ben? We don't have much time and all plans have to change. I suspect Pandit will be visiting us soon. The man up there has a sniper rifle all set up.'

'Yaakov should be able to deal with that problem,' commented Ben and Gautam nodded.

'Let me get the equipment out and organize my people. We'll discuss the details at breakfast.'

Fifteen minutes after Gautam left, Yaakov began to move. He scouted every step before he took it, putting his feet down carefully and noiselessly. His target having assembled his weapon, was motionless.

'Fucker's good!' said Yaakov to himself as he moved slowly towards Ram Singh, the Glock provided by Gautam in his left hand, a large stone in his right. The objective was to disable not kill, unless absolutely essential. Yaakov was ambidextrous and could shoot almost as accurately with his left as with his right hand. When he was about six feet behind and a little above his target and about to jump, Ram Singh sensed danger and moved very rapidly. He grabbed his rifle with his right hand and rolled to his left attempting to bring the long gun to bear on the threat he felt behind him.

A sniper rifle, however, is not designed for close quarter combat, especially one fully deployed and covered with a bit of sacking as camouflage. Besides, Yaakov was twenty years younger and poised to spring.

Yaakov dropped the gun and leapt on the recumbent Ram Singh and as he landed on him swung the stone hard at his head. Since the target was moving away, the blow was not enough to knock him out, but just enough to disorient the sniper for a moment. For Yaakov, a moment was enough. He dropped Ram Singh unconscious with a second hard knock to the side of the head, tied him up with plastic ties, repositioned the rifle and settled down to wait.

Gautam retrieved handguns and satphones from a large carefully constructed and concealed storage space and brought them into the drawing room.

He handed a Glock, two loaded mags, a box of ammo and a satphone to Ben and quickly outlined his plan for dealing with Pandit when he came.

'He's sent his man with a long gun early this morning, so I'm expecting him sometime in the forenoon. Grab a quick breakfast, Ben—I can hear Bahadur in the kitchen—and be on your way as planned. And remember, no risks. Keep your distance and keep me advised, that's it. Clear? Incidentally, Yaakov has confirmed he has command of the high ground—his text came in when I was getting this stuff out.'

Ben nodded and went to the kitchen to confer with the cook. Gautam called Joshiji on the intercom he had installed between the house and the cottage and gave clear instructions, overruled the inevitable protests, and sat down to the breakfast Bahadur had produced. Ben departed soon after and Gautam had a long chat with the cook about the disposal of the would-be assassin up on the ridge. He then strapped on a bulletproof vest—one of the several gifted to him by the Americans he had worked with on a drug-related op soon after retirement. He placed a .22 Beretta in an ankle holster, a Glock in a hip holster, put on a loose corduroy jacket and sat down on the verandah with a mug of coffee.

Bahadur took the dogs for a quick walk and then confined them indoors. They protested, but to no avail. Gautam did not want distractions this morning. Then Sher Bahadur Thapa, formerly of the 9 Para Commandoes, went back to his little cottage and made his own preparations. Colonel Sahib had his ideas about things, but he had also taught them about planning, preparedness and initiative. And he had taught well.

Gautam finished his coffee, rinsed out the mug in the kitchen sink, then sat down to prepare for what was to come.

'Preparing for combat is something you build into your system—it is always part of you. Of course, if you have the time you add to it—you quieten the mind, you heighten awareness, you abandon all concern about results. It is a meditative state and all the new age nonsense about meditation does not change that. Just be quiet; you are highly trained. All you have to do is get yourself out of the way and let It fight.'

The sensei's words echoed in Gautam's head as he sat waiting.

The morning drifted away quietly. The usual sounds of a small estate at work were absent. There was nobody chopping wood or hammering away at some recalcitrant metal contraption in the workshop. The dogs were not to be seen and even the monkeys seemed to have taken the day off from raiding the experimental patch of corn Gautam had planted on three terraces in a corner of the estate.

Around noon, the sound of a heavy diesel engine working its way slowly up the hill to the estate was heard.

Gautam took a deep breath, got up and strolled out to stand in the sun on the kuccha road that came up to his front porch.

18

When Pandit drove up to Gautam's place with his two henchmen, he found the gates wide open and no sign of either Joshiji or the two boys who worked on the estate. Driving up to the house, Pandit looked around with satisfaction at the cultivated terraces, the young fruit trees and the vegetable and herb gardens. A good deal, he thought; the buyer will be happy.

Then he saw Gautam, standing relaxed, in front of the house and for a fleeting moment felt a touch of disquiet. It all seemed to be going too easily. He shook his head impatiently. One retired fauji was really no match for him and his teams. He just had to be tougher with the fellow, no more slack—he signed today or went to hospital.

'Good morning, Colonel Sahib,' Pandit spoke jovially, as he got out of the SUV carrying a sheaf of legal-looking papers.

'Here are the papers, sir, and here is the cheque; and Jiten has a pen for you to sign with. I hope you are all packed and ready to leave, for your time has run out here.'

Gautam smiled slightly. 'I'm afraid I've changed my mind. I'm not leaving after all. In fact…' in mid-sentence Gautam's right hand flickered in a quick movement over his right hip and appeared holding the Glock, which was pointed at Pandit, center mass. 'You are the one leaving. Or you can die here, I don't really care which. But, you will never threaten me or anyone connected to me again. If you do, I will hunt you down and kill you and all your men. And believe me, you will not see me coming. This is the only warning you get. Decide quickly.'

Pandit took a few seconds to process this unexpected turn of events. He then laughed, easily, unaffectedly and raised his hands slowly to shoulder height.

'Easy boys, stay still—guns have a nasty way of going off when pointed, so don't move at all. I'm impressed, Colonel, sir, truly. I did not think you had it in you, but obviously what I was told about you was correct. You are tough, very tough indeed, and I admire you for it. But nothing changes, sirji, nothing at all. Please watch carefully now.'

Pandit raised his right hand above his head and waved. A small red dot appeared on the ground at Gautam's feet.

'You should recognize that for what it is, Colonel. It's the laser sight fixed to a sniper rifle overlooking this area. If you do not put your gun down, you will be dead very shortly. My man on the ridge is a very good shot and I'm sure you do not want to die today—such a lovely day too—or do you?'

'I don't,' replied Gautam. 'The question is do you and your men want to? Die today, I mean?'

Gautam waved his left hand and the red dot moved slowly to settle on Pandit's chest and stayed there.

Gautam shifted his gun to point at Jiten.

'The sniper now holding the rifle up there is also a very good shot. Between the two of us we will gun you down before you can get to those handguns you have in your jacket pockets. So choose, and quickly—my friend up there is not as patient as I am.'

Pandit stood silent and motionless, as did his men.

'What do you want, Colonel?' Pandit said finally, his voice only a trifle shaky with fury or fear, or perhaps both.

'I want all of you to carefully, with two fingers, take out all weapons you are carrying, one by one, and put them on the ground and take two steps back. Slowly now.'

The three complied, carefully. The red dot remained on Pandit's chest throughout.

'Now, get out of here and remember if any of my people are impacted in any way, I will come hunting. And as you have noticed, I have friends who have seen you clearly. So just go away and stay away from me and mine. Am I clear?'

Pandit had recovered what little composure he had lost. He chuckled softly—to all the world enjoying a small joke with friends.

'Wonderful! I seriously underrated you, Colonel Sa'ab, and I'll not make that mistake twice. For now, I will leave. Come on boys—we've learnt a lesson today and we have to digest it carefully.'

He tossed a mocking salute at Gautam, got into his Scorpio, and Jiten drove them away.

As soon as the vehicle was out of sight, Gautam spoke to Ben and Yaakov on the satphones.

'They have left, Ben. You ready for them?'

'Sure. I'm on the main road and will follow them at a distance and keep you posted on which way they go from the T-junction at Raiagar.'

'Good. I'll be behind you and as soon as Yaakov comes off the ridge, he will follow. Keep in touch guys. I'm moving now.'

'I'll be at my bike in fifteen minutes, Colonel,' replied Yaakov.

Gautam ended the call, stowed a loaded haversack and a stuffed duffel in his Gypsy and started the chase.

19

Sanju took a careful sip of the drink Datta had poured for him, set the glass down on a nearby table, and sprawled comfortably in his favourite armchair in Datta's study.

'What's bothering you?' asked Datta. 'Something is, that much is evident.'

Sanju laughed. 'O wise and discerning One, I am just a little uneasy with these French ladies. I checked up on them with various friends and the Brits told me the younger one has done considerable time undercover—in Syria, for heaven's sake—and the older one has a rather bloody history, too. So, I wonder just what are these wet work specialists doing here? God, that sounds like a dialogue out of a Bourne movie, doesn't it? But my concern is real—these people are not needed for the work that is to be done here. They know by now that we are quite capable of dealing with any rough stuff that may be required, so why send such operatives? And did you notice that Farah joined Didi much later and Didi seemed a trifle upset about it? Things don't add up, bro. I'm not comfortable.'

'To impress the President, perhaps? Remember the father of the girl is an old pal of the big boss. Maybe the head of the French Service is simply sucking up—'I've sent my best people sir, no stone will be left unturned blah blah blah…'

Sanju shook his head and reached for his glass. 'You and I both know that crusty old bastard doesn't work like that! Not his style to waste two high-class agents in this routine task. So, exactly what are they tasked with? I don't like it at all, not at all.'

'You'd better keep a close watch on them, then. Make sure they don't fuck about in our parish.'

'Sure, I will. Let's see what happens.'

Datta nodded and rose to his feet. 'I think Annie and Reena are back. Let's move to the sitting room, Sanju. Bring the bottle along, please. No more business to discuss, right?'

'Nope,' replied Sanju, picking up his glass and the bottle and following Datta out of the room. 'We wait and watch, for now.'

20

Pandit was silent, staring pensively out of the window as they drove away from Gautam's estate, down the kuccha road to the main road a couple of kilometres downhill.

'Where to boss?' asked Jiten, when they reached the blacktop.

'Let's go check up on the foreigners first. Then we'll go up the road and see what Pradeep has found. He said he's picked up some very promising stuff.'

Jiten drove fast and expertly along the winding hill road and Pandit remained thoughtful and silent for a long time.

'That Colonel is smarter than I expected and far too composed for my liking,' he said, breaking the silence finally. 'But what he did today does not make sense, no sense at all. So what was he trying to do?'

Pandit's henchmen remained quiet. They knew that when their boss was thinking aloud, he did not appreciate any disturbance whatsoever.

'He cannot imagine his play with guns will change anything, for fuck's sake. If he had shot us right there, yes, the problem would have been over; but he let us go with some silly dramatic dialogue. That doesn't solve anything and he is smart enough to know that. But forget the guesswork, let's stick to facts,' continued Pandit. 'He showed he has friends who can take out Ram Singh in the jungle and can handle a sniper rifle expertly. Now where can he find such friends in the interior Kumaon? Nobody has driven up to his place—we've been watching, right? That means someone walked up there and so, that somebody is a local man. And maybe there is more than one, let's consider all possibilities.'

Another couple of kilometres of driving later, Pandit suddenly smiled and smacked Jiten on the shoulder. 'So, where are local people with such warlike skills located in this part of the mountains, eh? Come on, you bastards, do I have to do all the thinking here?'

Jiten was not a local lad and so kept quiet. Alok, the other young tough accompanying Pandit, did, however, belong to the Berinag area and after some thought spoke up tentatively.

'Those Israeli fellows in Tinauli, sir; they are the only ones I can think of in the area. All Israelis have to do military service I'm told, and those young fellows are actually very tough; I've met one of them. A cousin of mine is a good friend of the chap called Yaakov. But they don't get involved in local matters, sir, usually. They stick to their farming and stuff, mind their own business.' Alok trailed off uncertainly.

Pandit nodded approvingly. 'Good thought. I cannot think of anyone else, and not just in this area either. It has to be them. So next step, what do we do about it? And what is the Colonel planning, eh? Tell me what is he planning with his little Jewish band? What can he possibly plan for?'

Ben had followed Pandit and his cohorts at a safe distance from the time they joined the main road. He was very familiar with the route and knew they would have to drive up to the crossing at Raiagar and then turn either right towards Berinag or left towards Almora. Three odd kilometres before the crossing point, Ben planned to overtake them, reach Raiagar, and hang back in a friend's shop to watch which direction they chose. This he would report to Gautam and Yaakov and hand over the task of following thereon to them.

The plan was clear and simple, but it overlooked two important issues. The first was that hill roads are winding, full of twists and turns and very often, if one is alert and observant, one can look back and see a vehicle on a turn a fair distance away. The second and very important factor was that Pandit, despite the recent setback at Gautam's, was alert and observant.

'A strange thing,' he mused thoughtfully, 'that neither of you clowns have cared to notice, is the fact that soon after we came down to the main road from the Colonel's place, there has been a motorcycle behind us and the driver has not tried to overtake us till now.'

'Lots of bikes on these roads now, boss,' observed Jiten, carefully. 'Locals and tourists both.'

'Yes, of course,' said Pandit. 'But again, which biker drives so carefully for so long, eh? Quite strange, but might well be nothing. Speed up a little and let's see what he does.'

Jiten accelerated and the biker evidently did so too, because the bike drew closer. Ben was simply sticking to his plan to overtake close to the crossing, which was just a few kilometres away.

'Now slow down,' ordered Pandit and as Jiten complied, Ben caught up, and with some aggressive hooting and acceleration, overtook the SUV and raced ahead.

'That was a local number plate,' observed Pandit. 'And we don't have bike rentals for tourists yet, do we?'

'No boss,' replied Jiten, 'not that I know of.'

'Er, boss, the Israelis have mobikes,' said Alok, hesitantly. 'And that driver looked a little like one of them, but I'm not sure.'

Pandit nodded, thought for a while and then resumed his loud thinking. 'I have two matters on hand, right. One is to finalize the exchange of the Frenchies for money and the other is to sort out this fucking fauji. But to do that we need to know what he is up to. Is he using the Israelis or are we just jumping at shadows? Let's try and confirm that and then finish the exchange of the firangis. Then we can come back and fix the Colonel aaram se.' Pandit paused his monologue and looked at his boys.

'Am I clear till now fellows? Anything you don't understand?'

The boys remained silent.

'Good. So let's try and confirm this Israeli involvement and then move to Almora and tomorrow to the farm to finish up that business. Jiten turn towards Berinag at the T-junction and let us see what happens.

'Also ask Sharmaji in Haldwani to check up the ownership details of the bike that just overtook us. Did anyone care to take down its number?'

Alok carefully recited the registration details.

Pandit nodded approvingly. 'I would have kicked your arse if you hadn't. They have it all computerized, so it should be no problem for him. Tell him I want it immediately, by this evening. He should text me the details.'

'I'm at Raiagar and will tell you which way Pandit's SUV goes. Then one of you can take up the trail and I will keep twenty minutes behind him,' said Ben on the satphone to Gautam and Yaakov.

'Don't be seen by them. Be careful,' advised Gautam. 'I've let Yaakov get ahead of me. I'll be ten minutes behind him. Give me status reports every five minutes. Don't underrate these people, they are pros.'

'Sure, Colonel,' replied Yaakov. 'I'm speeding up and will be just five odd minutes behind them from the junction.'

Pandit and team drove through Raiagar and turned towards Berinag. Neither of them spotted Ben, who was watching through the grimy window of a teashop. Nor did they see his bike concealed behind the same shop and out of sight of the road.

Yaakov took up position a safe distance behind Pandit's SUV and Gautam followed a good way behind.

'This part of the hills is suddenly full of motorcycles,' observed Pandit abruptly.

'The same one boss?' asked Jiten.

'How the fuck would I know? All I see is a bike some way behind us. Ok, if the Colonel has got his friends following us, let's get it clear one way or another. Stop in that wooded stretch two kilometres down the road, Jiten.'

'Yes, boss. But there is traffic on the road, boss—not much, but fairly regular traffic.'

Pandit turned and looked at his driver. 'We do stop at that naula to drink water often, right? And just by the way, I have no intention of warning the good Colonel that we are on to him, if indeed this biker is one of his people.'

Jiten looked questioningly at his boss, who shook his head impatiently. 'I can simply shoot him and throw him into the ravine there, but then the Colonel will know we know he is having us followed. Do you understand or is it too complicated for you? I just want to confirm whether it is one of the Israelis or not. If yes, we know they are coming after us and can prepare for them; if not, all is well. Understood?'

Jiten nodded.

'So just park at the naula and Alok and I will get out to drink water and confirm the biker's identity. That's all.'

Yaakov rounded a sharp bend and saw the SUV parked by the side of the road and Pandit and one of his men at the spring by the roadside. Stopping short would have given the game away, so he decided to press on and drove by the parked vehicle without altering speed or showing any curiosity about the SUV or its passengers.

'It's him, the Israeli called Yaakov,' said Alok to Pandit. 'The helmet cannot conceal his build, and it's his bike alright. No question boss, it's him.'

Pandit nodded. 'Good, the Colonel was being clever. All that drama was just to be able to track us to our base and then, maybe, come after us. Very good. So now we know and can get back to focusing on our first priority—the exchange. Turn around and head back to Almora. Let's see if anyone follows us and actually has the balls to try any funny business on Almora Mall Road, eh?'

Yaakov drove for five minutes after passing Pandit's SUV, stopped and called Gautam.

'Do you think he spotted and identified you?' asked Gautam.

'I think so. One of the chaps with him is some relative of a friend of mine and I've met him once. If they are as smart as you think they are, they must have spotted me and stopped to confirm.'

'Yes, they are smart. No matter. Wait a while to see what they do. I'm stopping too, so we have them bracketed. Let's see what they do and decide our course of action from that.'

Gautam found a kuchha track taking off from the main road—one of many village roads on which work starts, but stops due to non-availability of funds— and carefully backed his Gypsy onto it till the vehicle was out of eyeshot from the main road. He then took out a pair of binoculars from his backpack, found a spot from where he could see the road and settled down to wait and watch.

About ten minutes later, he saw Pandit's SUV approaching, and when it had passed him, he called Yaakov and asked him to come back and meet him at Raiagar. He called Ben and asked him to wait at Raiagar where they would join him.

'I'll trail them and see what happens. You two find out where they may have a base. It is obviously in this area. Just try and get information—everybody knows everything about everybody else in these parts. But do nothing, ok? No scouting around. Get info and we'll check out any leads together when I'm back from wherever I'm going now.'

Gautam rolled into Raiagar to find his two young collaborators waiting by the crossing.

'If you intend to follow him, Colonel, you should change vehicles. Your red Gypsy is visible from afar and it will be daylight for quite some time yet,' observed Ben.

Gautam nodded. 'True, but I have no option here.'

'Actually, you do,' replied Yaakov. 'A friend of mine has a taxi, a Maruti Alto, which is in very good shape despite its age. He maintains it himself and is surprisingly good at it. And it's available for your use right away.'

'Here and now?' asked Gautam.

'Absolutely, Colonel. You see, he lives just down the road and tripped and twisted his ankle the other day. It's swollen up like a balloon and there's no way he can drive for a while. He would be thrilled to rent it out to you—it's just sitting there not earning anything otherwise. I've spoken to him and we can change over now and leave your Gypsy here. We'll be here and you won't be away for very long?'

'No I don't think so. But, we'll see and coordinate on phone. So let's get on with it. I don't want to lose them.'

The Alto was in very good shape for a hill taxi and Gautam drove way faster than he normally did. He caught sight of Pandit's vehicle halfway up the mountain after crossing the river at Seraghat. He slowed down and maintained his position ten minutes behind his quarry.

Pandit stopped at Barechhina and Gautam drove past to 'trail from the front' all the way to the outskirts of Almora, where he let them overtake him, fell in a little way behind them, until they drove into the town. The lower mall road was crowded and he followed them to a large house—an imposing concrete monstrosity in a sea of similar, though smaller, structures—where Pandit got off.

Almora used to be a pretty, small town high up on a ridge with a magnificent view of the high Himalayas but 'modernization and development' had converted it into a filthy concrete sprawl. Gautam wondered at the ability of population pressure, incompetent town planners and corrupt bureaucracy to destroy and degrade everything nature had to offer.

The SUV moved off and Gautam followed, a tentative plan of action germinating in his mind. The vehicle stopped to let off Alok, and Jiten drove on alone, oblivious of the dusty little car closing up behind him.

21

'Himalaya Burning' screamed the headlines in a major English language national daily. 'Summer Forest Fires Ravage Kumaon' yelled another.

Sanju tossed the newspapers on the table in disgust. 'Every fucking year it's the same story, Fatso, every fucking year. And nobody can do anything at all!'

Datta picked up the paper and scanned the headlines. 'The paper mills need wood, Sanju, and the Forest Department can legitimately auction every dead tree in the forest. So, we have lots of dead trees for auction in the forests every year. I just hope Buddha's area is clear. The pre-monsoons should hit the hills soon, and that should help. And finally, the monsoon will take care of the fires, as usual.'

'You are a cynical bastard, Fatso, totally!' replied Sanju.

'The wisdom to know what you cannot change, Sanju, is the greatest of all wisdoms,' said Datta in a deep, serious tone of voice.

Sanju laughed. 'Sure, O Wise One, but it hurts, that's all. Anyway, call Buddha and check if his place is ok.'

Ten minutes later the friends gave up trying to connect to Gautam.

'He's obviously moving. The connection is lousy on

the rare occasion that it actually connects. Forget it, I'll try at night,' said Datta and the conversation turned to other matters.

'We traced the cellphone from which the ransom demand was made and the video sent. Belongs to a young executive of a consulting company working in Gurugram. They stole her handbag from her car, used the phone and tossed it by the time she got an FIR registered. Very slick work—these guys are smart. But we have one slim lead. We know the gang that specializes in such thefts and I'm getting some of them rounded up. I'll have a chat with them this evening and see if any lead emerges.'

Datta looked warningly at his friend. 'For God's sake, take care, Sanju. Don't get into trouble again. These guys have connections in very high places, starting with your worthy department.'

Sanju smiled. 'Now you're telling me about my department, Fatso? Remember I've done this in Bihar for ten years and you haven't seen politicized policemen until you've seen the cops in my home state, bro. Relax. Waterboarding, Saran style, leaves no marks! No scars, no trace, no harm, no foul! I'll let you know if this yields anything useful.'

22

Farah went for a run in Nehru Park early morning, while Didi worked through a one-and-half-hour t'ai chi routine on the lawn of the French Embassy guesthouse where they were staying. By eight, they were both down for breakfast in the dining room.

'The waiting getting to you?' asked Didi.

Farah nodded and helped herself to a hot croissant and a cup of coffee.

'This hanging around all day is painful. Too hot to go looking at monuments and there's no shooting range either.'

Didi smiled. 'I would have thought you got enough practice in recent months.'

'I did, but it's a good way to pass the time,' replied Farah.

'Yes. Oh, by the way, Mr Datta has invited us to dinner tonight, at his home. I've said yes for both of us.'

Farah raised her shapely eyebrows. 'His home?'

'Yes, apparently that's his style—personal and informal. At least, that's what his file said,' replied Didi. 'We didn't have time to brief you in detail as you were assigned at the very last minute.'

'Yes, it was a mad rush catching the flight. But tell me about these guys; they appear to be clever, but not very hard. How effective are they?'

Didi got up to refill her coffee mug. 'Don't get taken in by the style and all this "come meet the family at my home" bonhomie. That Datta is both clever and cold, and Sanjay has a reputation for getting his hands dirty in difficult ops, unlike other Indian officers.'

'You mentioned that they executed some messy projects recently with the Israelis and the Americans. You have the details?'

'Not too many, but what we have looks very impressive. They, Datta and team, took out a drug lord, who also happened to be a senior Member of their Parliament, and soon thereafter, another drug kingpin trying to set up opium poppy cultivation on a large scale in the mountains. They have a friend—a retired Special Forces colonel, apparently—who did most of the dirty work. He has quite a rep that colonel, but we haven't met him yet.'

'Retired colonels need a battalion of infantry and artillery support to get anything done, Didi!' said Farah with a sniff, as she replenished her coffee cup.

'Oh, I don't know,' replied Didi. 'This one apparently is a fourth Dan black belt. Given by Sensei K himself, supposedly the greatest living exponent of the art. Also, he was embedded with the US Special Forces in Afghanistan for a three-month tour—recon and interdiction on the Af-Pak border. Rough stuff that must have been. The Yanks apparently were very impressed. At least, that's what my sources told me. It would be interesting to meet him, if he comes on this job.'

'Better if he doesn't, no; much easier without such hard cases around,' observed Farah.

'Yes, true, but it would add some spice to the exercise. Let's see. Now let's go shopping—everything is air conditioned, don't worry, and I've no clothes for socializing. Datta did say casual informal, but what the hell, we have our national reputation for chic to maintain!'

~

The Frenchwomen reached Datta's house at 7.30 p.m. and were soon overwhelmed by Annie's charm. Datta's English wife, clad in a casual but chic cotton salwar kurta, was genuinely warm, friendly and welcoming, without being intrusive or overbearing.

'I thought you might like an Indian meal, without the chillies, of course, but if you find it difficult, I make a mean omelette and I've baked some baguettes just this morning,' said Annie, as Datta served Didi a whiskey soda and Farah a gin and tonic.

'Oh, I'll go with the Indian food,' exclaimed Farah. 'And I can handle a fair amount of chillies, too.'

'Same here,' said Didi. 'There's a small Indian restaurant near my house and I'm a regular customer. And I always ask for their red chillies fried in ghee as add-on. They keep that for those who can handle hot food.'

Annie got to her feet quickly. 'I'll tell the cook to make up a small bowl of mirchi-ghee to spice things up a bit.'

'Its very kind of you to call us over, Datta,' said Didi, after tasting her drink and nodding approval.

Datta smiled and offered a bowl of cashew nuts to the guests. 'Restaurants are too public for people like us, Didi, and the food's better at home, anyway. Sanju will be here soon and he might have a lead—a slender one, he says, but a lead of sorts. Something to do while we wait for the kidnappers to get in touch about the exchange.'

Sanju arrived an hour later. The party was well on its way, second drinks were being finished and the atmosphere was relaxed and congenial. Annie and Didi had discovered a common passion for Van Gogh and were comparing the collection at the Van Gogh Museum in Amsterdam with that at the New York's MOMA, while Datta was discussing EU politics with a surprisingly animated and well-informed Farah.

Sanju made straight for the bar and joined the group with a large whiskey in hand.

'Sorry for being late, people. We had a lead, but some work was needed to flesh out the details. We have an idea about the person who was contracted for the cellphones that were used to talk to Paris. I should have some more news tomorrow.'

'That was quick,' remarked Didi approvingly. 'Do you mind giving us some details?'

'Not at all,' replied Sanju. He polished off his drink and made himself another before he continued.

'Both cellphones were stolen from Gurugram, from people resident and working in the city. There is just one very well-organized gang doing this, so we rounded up the leaders—two brothers run that show—and persuaded them to tell us who commissioned the theft. It was a long shot, but they came up with interesting info. Apparently, the same man asked for high-end phones on two occasions. They gave us the details of the phones and we found that they were the same ones from which the calls were made to France. And best of all, he let slip that he will need one more soon—he will let them know when. One of my boys is with them 24/7 and when the demand is placed, we will supply the phone and be there at the handover. If the buyer is a member of the kidnapping gang and not just a cut-out being handled at arms' length, we will have serious actionable info. In any case, he will tell us all he knows and we'll proceed from there.'

Sanju paused to pick up a handful of cashew nuts, took a swallow of his drink and slumped in a deep armchair.

After a moment, Didi softly clapped her hands. 'Bravo, Sanjay. That was good work.'

Sanju smiled. 'More luck than anything else, but luck helps. These gangs are smart—they keep the numbers and sim details of the phones they peddle, just in case. That's how we matched them to the calls to Paris.'

'Luck does help, doesn't it,' observed Datta. 'I think this calls for a quick last one before dinner, folks.' He looked at his guests, both of whom nodded acceptance after a brief hesitation.

The party ended by eleven and the French officers were back in their guesthouse half an hour later.

'That Sanjay is a smart guy,' observed Farah. 'Moves fast too.'

Didi shrugged. 'Nothing we can do at present except wait, Farah. That last drink got to me, it did. Let's get some sleep. Goodnight.'

23

Gautam drank water from the bottle he carried, ate two energy bars and after night fell, took a long piss by the side of the road. The rest of the time he stayed still about fifty yards away from the house where Jiten had parked and gone in. The house was at the other end of Almora where the old toll house used to be back in the day.

Around ten o'clock, Jiten emerged and, walking just a trifle unsteadily, got into the SUV and drove off downhill. Gautam followed, keeping fairly close as there was traffic on the road and he didn't want to lose Jiten in the dark.

Down the hill went Jiten and then after crossing a venerable old iron girder bridge almost at the bottom of the mountain, he turned left, up a new road that connected Bhowali with Almora via Ramgarh. The traffic on this road was sparse and Gautam held back a little so as not to alert him.

Twenty minutes along, Jiten stopped at a small village that straddled the road in a typical hilly style—houses on both sides of the road with teashops and restaurants dominating the roadside and closed for the night. The house he stopped at was a little beyond the main village and awash with light; music floated out of curtained windows and a couple of battered SUVs and an elderly Maruti 800 were parked alongside on the road. Gautam drove on, turned around, parked out of sight of the house and walked back. He settled himself to observe from the shadows of a gnarled old tree that had surprisingly survived by the roadside and soon realized that he was surveilling a rather popular brothel. Traffic for the house of joy—local taxis each carrying several passengers—was regular, though not heavy, and slowed down around midnight, which was when Jiten emerged and made for his Scorpio. At the sight of him, Joshiji's broken fingers flashed in Gautam's mind—the old man had described Jiten very accurately—and he had to take a moment to quieten himself, as he watched him stroll up to his vehicle.

Jiten was parked about twenty paces beyond the house. He had come out obviously a satisfied man, smiling, humming a popular film ditty, chewing paan and smelling powerfully of cheap whiskey, and gently of cheap perfume. He fumbled in his pocket for the car keys, started unlocking the door, remembered he hadn't locked it in the first place and swung it open and clambered in. As he settled himself and inserted the key in the ignition, there was a sharp rap on the front passenger side window.

'Wha', who the fuck are you, man?' he asked of the man outside his window. 'You want a lift, you cheap bastard? Can't pay for the ride, eh? Chhamiya made you pay for her rides, eh?' Jiten laughed, leaned across and unlocked the passenger side door. 'Come on then, get in, I'm in a good mood today, otherwise I would kick your arse for bothering me. Might still kick it if you are a chutia. Get in, I'm going to Almora, ok? Upto the toll house only, you can fucking walk thereafter, cheap bastard. Get in, get in, busy day tomorrow, need to get my beauty sleep.'

The passenger side door opened, the dark figure outside leaned in and said softly, 'You shouldn't beat up old men, Jiten. Not good for your health.'

Through the light fog of alcohol and post-coital contentment, Jiten realized that something was seriously amiss, but his reaction was a trifle slow. A hard, metallic item pressed into his chest and two small, muffled explosions drove two .22 bullets into his heart. Jiten, startled and afraid, was dead before he knew it.

~

Gautam drove slowly through a sleeping Almora and on towards Raiagar. It had been a very long day and he was tired.

A tea shop in Barechhina was open to serve the night buses that connected interior Kumaon with the plains and Gautam stopped to down two mugs of the hot, sweet over-boiled concoction that masqueraded as tea at such shops and drove on into the night. Yaakov and Ben were waiting at Raiagar when Gautam rolled in early morning and they sat down to talk over hot parathas at what Ben called the best roadside dhaba in the mountains.

'We did some asking around, Colonel, and we have some rather slender leads,' reported Ben. 'Nobody, not even my friends, want to talk about Pandit. But then, I've been around here from before he started up, so some things do come out, out of the corner of the mouth, so to speak. Anyway, a local boy from a village down the road has joined Pandit's gang some time ago. Bright fellow he was, but had a cold, nasty streak in him; Alok is his name. A while ago, he bought a small house a short distance from here, off the Berinag road. He doesn't live there, but people from the gang have been observed around here, passing through, buying provisions, booze and stuff. You know the hills, Colonel. Everyone knows what's happening despite the distances and the isolation, at least in general terms, the broad outlines as it were. For example, the house is occupied now, although Alok drove through towards Almora just yesterday—a cousin of his spotted him and the grocery shop by the corner sold a lot of provisions to some strangers a few days ago—pahari boys, rough lot, but not local. Thin info, sir, but enough to justify some reconnaissance time.'

Gautam nodded thoughtfully. 'I need to get home and get some sleep and I want to go with you tonight to check things out, so spend the day here probing further; but don't arouse any suspicions, please. And get some rest, too, it may well be a long night. I'll call when I start from home. I'll take my Gypsy now and we'll meet a kilometre outside this place and drive through in the dark. As you said, too many eyes here.'

Gautam was home half an hour later and asleep fifteen minutes thereafter. Those fifteen minutes were, however, difficult. Killing in war is hard enough despite all the training and the emotional hype, but gunning down a half-drunk goon for a bit of casual and relatively minor violence raised disturbing questions that agitated his mind; but he pushed them aside, to deal with later. He slept for eight hours, had a leisurely hot bath, a light meal, and then prepared for the night ahead.

Ben and Yaakov dallied over endless cups of tea at a friend's dhaba and when the settlement was awake and functional, they went their separate ways. Ben had many good friends, Yaakov, a few very good ones, and they spent the day hanging out in their own particular ways, looking for scraps of information to support the basic data they had got the day before. They let it be known that they were simply taking a couple of days off from their hard routine and chilling in the traditional local style—dawdling over tea in various tea shops, gossiping about local affairs and generally doing nothing much at all.

24

Pandit woke early and called Ashok at the cottage where the French couple were being held. 'I want you to get the foreigners to the farm tonight and I want you to pass through Haldwani after dark—I don't want them spotted. Start off after lunch, a late start, take them to the farm and hold them there. Don't let them be seen en route—especially in the towns, Almora and Bhowali. Run through these places, carry packed lunch, eat on the run and pee by the roadside. Take the Almora-Ramgarh-Bhowali road and call me when you are at the farm.'

He then waited for Jiten to arrive with the SUV.

Sharmaji from the Road Transport Office in Haldwani called and confirmed that the motor cycle registration number he had been given was in the name of Yaakov Rubenstein, a resident of village Tinauli, district Almora.

'Clever, Colonel Saheb, to use these boys, but not clever enough,' mused Pandit. 'And for that, I'm going to wipe them out and bury them in their damn forests. And you too, Colonel, once you have signed off that beautiful property. Now where is that fucking Jiten! Time I gave him a serious kicking to bring back some discipline.'

At nine, a terrified Chhamiya called to inform him that Jiten was lying dead in the Scorpio, shot twice through the heart by a small calibre weapon. Chhamiya was smart and well educated in the nuts and bolts of the criminal world. She was an enterprising spirit from the terai, financed in part by Pandit in her high-profit venture and protected from venal policemen and other such dangers also by Pandit.

'Who else knows?' asked Pandit.

'Everybody,' wailed the lady. 'Some boys about their morning business discovered him, informed the patwari, who lives in the next village and he must be there by now. Now they'll question me for days and ruin business completely.'

'Just tell them the truth—he came, he had a drink and left. Did anyone—your boys and girls—see anything? Anything at all?'

'I asked. One of my girls did see a battered old taxi leave towards Almora soon after he left. She assumed it was Jiten—she is new, doesn't know about the Scorpio.'

'It was not a taxi running through?'

'No, I questioned her carefully. She heard it start and then drive off carefully. It was a small Maruti and not new, she says. She's a Haldwani girl—knows her cars.'

'Ok. Deal with it at arm's length. And don't think this reduces your monthly contribution either. Don't try to be clever with me, Chhamiya, it doesn't work and causes pain, a lot of pain.'

Pandit ended the call, called Alok, told him to collect another vehicle from the garage—another business enterprise he owned and used to good effect—and sat back to think.

He sat with a cup of tea and started to work things out. A few minutes of thought and the conclusions were obvious. The Colonel had followed them after switching cars—the Jews had friends in the area—waited for an opportunity and taken Jiten out. The message was loud and clear and so was Pandit's future course of action. Once the foreign couple was exchanged for ransom, the Colonel had to be eliminated—simple survival strategy. The man was seriously dangerous and had to be removed from play. But, business first, as always. As soon as Alok came with the vehicle, he would leave for the farm, personally supervise the hostage exchange, and then return to sort out the Colonel.

As instructed, Ashok and Billu started after a late lunch with the French couple for the farm beyond Haldwani near Rudrapur. At Raiagar, Ashok realized he had no booze and asked his young colleague to stop and buy a bottle to ease the tedium of the long drive. When Billu entered the local theka, Ben was ensconced in a corner munching on a bagful of peanuts and chatting with the owner, one of his many friends in the area. Billu bought a bottle and left, and a minute later the booze shop owner confided to Ben that Billu was another one of Pandit's boys and had been around for a couple of days in the area—or so he thought. Ben continued with the small talk for a brief while, then strolled out hoping desperately to catch a glimpse of Pandit's men and the vehicle they were in. He was lucky. Ashok had decided to stock up on some snacks, and following Pandit's orders to not stop at any of the big towns en route, had instructed Billu to pick up a bag of pakoras from a shop that was in the process of frying a large lot to meet the evening demand.

Ben called Yaakov and briefed him quickly, gave him the registration number of the SUV and told him to inform Gautam, while he, Ben, would follow Pandit's men.

'I have to rush, they are leaving and I have to get my bike from behind Daju's shop. Talk to the Colonel and let me know what he wants us to do.'

Ben retrieved his bike and chased after the SUV, while Yaakov called Gautam.

'Right then, let Ben follow them and keep us posted. Tonight, you and I will try to find their hideout. If we do, we can twist details of their operations from whoever is there. If no one's there, we'll follow Ben and take them wherever we find them. Just tell Ben to take care and maintain a safe distance. No contact till we catch up with him. I'll call you when I leave—it'll be after dark—and pick you up for our recce.'

'Yes, sir, Colonel Sahib. I'll meet you a kilometre before the crossing and I'll speak to Ben.'

25

'We're the only ones here, so if they are the kidnappers, they have another place or else have disposed of their victims already,' observed Ruth, when they were alone in their room after lunch.

'Yes. Let's not waste time. Let's extract whatever info we can out of this lot and move on. If the Colonel learns you have left Delhi and haven't reached him, he might throw an ing-bing,' said Dana.

'He doesn't know I am back, Dana. But if he gets to know…yes, I don't want to worry the poor boy,' said Ruth with a laugh.

'I'm not really worried about him, I'm worried about what he might do to anyone he thinks is responsible for your disappearance, Ruth,' said Dana dryly. 'He still wants to lead a normal life—poor chap—but he's not normal, is he? And if he goes berserk, he will damage his normal image and find it difficult to live the way he wants to; the fantasy of the country squire growing potatoes in the Himalayas and keeping his devils at bay by Zen meditation or whatever nonsense he's working with these days.'

'You're too cynical, Dana,' said Ruth with a grimace. 'His Buddhism thing is serious for him.'

'Yes, as is his karate and all those other martial arts he

has mastered. Martial arts are for fighting, Ruth, whatever patina of spirituality you may give them. He's a warrior, simple. I'm being polite and not using the word killer, because that's what we all are.'

Ruth shrugged. 'I disagree, but let's leave this argument for another time. So, we breakout now, get what info we can and move on to Gautam's place?'

'Yup— the old pain in the stomach routine? I'll be the sick one. And we take them out, right Ruth? No debate there?'

Ruth shook her head. 'They kidnap for a living, they suffer the consequences. But disposal has to be thought out, Dana.'

'Lot of jungle here,' replied Dana, 'and deep ravines. We'll manage. Let's do it after dinner.'

But nature took a hand in the matter before they could execute their plan. While dinner was in progress, the smell of smoke wafted down from the ridge above and soon their door banged open and a worried Pradeep barged in. 'We have to leave, ladies, immediately. A forest fire is sweeping down very fast towards us. I was hoping it would burn itself out—they often do—but this one is aggressive. Pack up, please, and come out—you have two minutes.'

He walked out leaving the door open.

The two women looked at each other.

'We go along, for now. May take us to the place where the others are. Let's see,' said Ruth. Dana nodded agreement and the two were out of the cottage very quickly.

The men were waiting, the vehicles loaded and the two-car convoy left in a hurry. The entire hillside above the cottage was in flames and the fire was sweeping down fast. The smell of forest burning, the smoke and the flames evoked a primal fear that left none untouched. Ruth drove her Jeep with Dana beside her and Pradeep in the back, while Pradeep's cohorts followed in their Scorpio. They came down the hill on the rough track far too fast, and once on the tarred road, sped towards Raiagar. Twenty minutes later, Pradeep told Ruth to slow down and then directed her up the hill on another kuchha track.

'Just a little way up the hill, ladies, and you are at our second resort,' said Pradeep, making an effort at being jovial and not quite succeeding.

They reached the 'resort' and found a much larger cottage with another elderly and concerned caretaker looking worriedly at the hillside above the building. There was no fire on the hill but a faint orange glow was visible in the sky above the ridgeline.

'Get inside, ladies, but don't unpack just yet. I don't like the look of things here,' instructed Pradeep brusquely, got out and conferred with the very concerned elder responsible for the 'resort'.

'The fire is close to the top of the mountain,' the old man, Bhim Singh by name, muttered. 'If it jumps the top, it will be here in a couple of hours. The hillside is dry.'

'Fuck! Let's hope it doesn't!' exclaimed Pradeep. 'Anyway, there's no need to panic just yet. Get some tea going and we'll wait and watch.'

An hour later, the fire did jump the crest of the ridge and Pradeep reached for his cellphone and dialed Pandit.

Pandit heard Pradeep out, thought for a while and gave clear instructions.

'Get away from the cottage, get rid of the women and their vehicle in a deep khudd and come down to the farm to reinforce the team there in the exchange of hostages for the ransom. I want that to go without any hitch. But remember, Pradeep, no bullet holes in the women or their gaadi—I don't want any fucking police enquiry finding anything but a tragic accident on our narrow mountain roads. Understood? Think you and your boys can manage a couple of women without cocking it up, eh?'

Pradeep laughed briefly; he was senior enough in Pandit's hierarchy to occasionally take such a liberty. 'I'll do my best, boss, and let you know as soon as we are on our way. I will be at the farm by morning.'

Gautam drove out after dark and picked up Yaakov as decided, a short way outside Raiagar.

'Spoke to Ben a short while ago, sir,' reported Yaakov. 'He's trailing them at a safe distance and they're headed for the plains, it appears. They've taken the Ramgarh road after Almora and are driving slow and careful. Also, there are reports of serious forest fires in the area we are supposed to check out tonight. A friend just drove in from that direction and said that it looks bad—multiple fires on the whole Raiagar-Berinag route and beyond.'

Gautam nodded. 'Let's take a look anyway. How far is this place you've heard of?'

'A fairly short drive on the main road and then up the hill for a bit. You know how the locals give directions. We'll just have to take a chance.'

'Fine, let's do that,' replied Gautam, engaged gears and drove on.

About half an hour beyond the Raiagar crossing, the forest fires became visible. The moon was almost full and the play of moonlight on the mountain landscape—normally a breathtakingly beautiful sight—was marred by the blazing vermillion of burning pine and oak forest. The smell wafted down to the road and as they drove on, smoke billowing down the mountain became visible.

'Bloody hell, Colonel, the wind is towards us and the nearest fire is obviously close. And we still haven't reached the turn off to this so-called cottage up the hill…'

Gautam braked to a halt and held up a hand for silence. 'Did you hear that?' he asked. 'Sounded like gunshots.'

'Yes, but forest fires generate all sorts of explosive sounds, boss…' Yaakov trailed off as a series of muted explosions were heard. 'Professional double taps from a handgun, I would say, Colonel, if it weren't slightly ridiculous in the context of a forest fire, where it's probably just bursting pine cones.'

Gautam shook his head. 'Too precise to be pine cones. Let's be ready for the worst, Yaakov.'

Gautam drove forward slowly with headlights switched off, while Yaakov, Glock in hand, peered into the darkness for hostiles.

~

'What was that conversation about?' muttered Ruth in Hebrew.

'Not clear, but doesn't sound good. They can't possibly have so many safe houses to stash kidnapees in, can they?' replied Dana.

'And if they don't, they can't just let us go—so…'

'Yeah, I think we should just end it now, Ruth. Dump them in the cottage and let the fire dispose of them.'

'Just hold on a while, but be ready for anything now,' instructed Ruth.

'Sure, but I'm getting uneasy here.'

'All right, ladies, get back in the vehicle, we have to move on. Come on, boys, get in—one of you with me and the ladies; the other follows us, quickly now. Let the old man be. He'll monitor the fire and get away if it comes too near. He knows all the shortcuts and will manage on his own.'

The fire reached the top of the ridge and began sweeping down rapidly as they drove off.

'Easy now, don't drop us in the ravine, woman,' snapped Pradeep, as Ruth sped downhill rather fast.

Dana and Ruth exchanged a quick glance. Dropping people in a ravine seemed to be uppermost in Pradeep's mind at the moment! They came to the road and drove in the direction of Raiagar.

Pradeep was familiar with the landscape and remembered a deep, steep-sided, lightly wooded ravine coming up on their left.

'All right, stop here, ladies, end of the road, I'm afraid,' said Pradeep and as the vehicle coasted to a halt, he and Harish reached forward to get chokeholds on the slender and very vulnerable looking feminine necks in front of them.

Ruth and Dana turned back together, both holding guns. Pradeep and his partner died instantly, each shot through the head, twice.

The girls stepped out of the vehicle and ran to the trailing SUV that had come to a confused stop close behind them. The driver died in a careful burst of gunfire—the professional double taps Gautam heard half a kilometre away.

Ruth and Dana dragged Pradeep and Harish to the SUV, stuffed them in, opened the lid of the fuel tank and pushed the vehicle over the edge of the road. The SUV toppled over, the girls returned to their vehicle, started up, switched on the headlights just as Gautam drove around the nearest turn and stopped.

'Shit,' muttered Ruth. 'Don't shoot, for heaven's sake, Dana. We have to talk our way out of this one somehow. We saw this vehicle swerving across the road and crashing through the guardrail and stopped to see if there's anything we can do. Simple and straightforward, right?'

'Looks like the Colonel's Gypsy, Ruth,' said Dana, rolled down her window and in a parade ground voice yelled, 'Is that you, Colonel, this is Dana and Ruth here, no constraints, so don't shoot us, please.'

Gautam switched on his headlights stepped out and from behind the cover of his open door yelled, 'Gautam here, Dana. Switch off your lights and step out.'

An explosion sounded deep in the ravine as Pradeep's vehicle caught fire and ten minutes later Gautam's Gypsy and Ruth's Jeep were driving off towards Raiagar and from there to Gautam's estate.

They had driven for just about ten minutes when the first pre-monsoon showers hit the area with a short but very heavy downpour.

26

Ben had to drive rather fast to catch up with Ashok's SUV, but after doing so, he dawdled along behind them, tanked up at Barechhina and took up a closer position as darkness fell. They drove through Almora without stopping and then took the Ramgarh road and made their way at a surprisingly moderate pace to Bhowali with just a pee break in the wilderness. As instructed, Ashok did not stop at Bhowali, but drove down through Bhimtal and onwards to Haldwani.

Ben reported his position regularly to Yaakov and learnt about the encounter with Dana and Ruth when approaching Haldwani.

'So what's the plan now?' he asked.

'We're all going to the Colonel's place to get a meal and some rest and then early morning we'll come up to wherever you are. You know the Colonel, he is flexible, doesn't over plan. Anyway, whatever he has in mind, he's not telling us at this point,' replied Yaakov.

'Well, I'm starving and these buggers are being very careful, not stopping anywhere, more or less. I'll try and grab a paratha roll from that fellow opposite Kathgodam station, let's see. I'll keep you posted.'

'Cool. The Colonel says not to get too close and once

they come to rest, tell us the location and keep back—no close contact at all. Ok?'

'Sure. I've got my old camera and telephoto lens, so I'll take some pictures as soon as it is light. I'm still not sure how many and who exactly are in the SUV.'

Pandit reached the farm well before Ashok did with his passengers, thought through the plan for the exchange and after dinner called his man in Gurugram.

'Get a new phone, call the Frenchies and tell them they must be ready as instructed with the money in two days when further instructions for the exchange will be given to them. This will keep them reassured and on edge at the same time. Then get another phone the day after and I'll give you further instructions to transmit. And Guddu, don't get greedy—toss each phone immediately after the conversation is over. Do not keep it or sell it or any such stupid thing. They can track phones in many ways now, remember that.'

Guddu placed his requisition with the 'mobile gang', as he called them, and the information was relayed to Sanju by his agent liaising with them.

'This Guddu wants a phone early tomorrow morning, sir,' reported Ismail, a seasoned field agent, who had worked with Sanju for several years. 'He also wants a fresh one two days from now.'

'Great, Ismail. Now you go over to Gurugram with your team—you've got the two you wanted, right? The tech guys have a phone ready—in fact, they have three ready—and you will personally hand over the phone posing as a member of the gang and then you three will follow this guy. We will listen to what he says and then we will pick him up—you people will do it—when I say so and bring him to the safe house in Aurangzeb Lane. Clear?'

Ismail's acknowledgement was monosyllabic—he was a quiet man.

'Good, get on with it and keep me posted,' said Sanju and ended the call.

Sanju called Datta to brief him and learnt that Gautam had just called and given a detailed report on happenings in the mountains.

'Bloody hell, things are moving right along aren't they! I'll start Bhanu Bisht, whom I've been holding in reserve, towards Haldwani right away. Connect him to the Israeli lad and get them to meet up. It's never good to have just one person doing a tail job—too risky. Still too many open issues, Fatso. I'll talk to G and let's see how things work out by morning. Picture should be clearer then. Call the French ladies for a meeting tomorrow morning at the safe house. If this Gurugram guy—calls himself Guddu, by the way—uses the cell to make the call in the morning, we should have him in the bag and talking before noon. Get things moving along. Brief you early tomorrow.'

'Right, Sanju. Leave you to it then,' said Datta and the conversation ended.

27

Gautam and Yaakov, followed by Ruth and Dana, reached Gautam's place, freshened up and sat down to talk. Sher Bahadur began working on a quick meal.

'I wanted to surprise you, G,' explained Ruth. 'And then I met Dana in Almora and thought I'd add the kidnappers—or at least information about them—to my surprise present for you. That's why we got a little delayed.'

Gautam shook his head in exasperation. 'Reckless, and for no reason, Ruth!'

'Ah, come on, Gautam! Dana and me, fully equipped, going up against a bunch of common or garden crooks is hardly reckless. Anyway, all's well that ends well and so forth. Now what is to be done?'

Gautam took a deep breath and smiled with a bit of effort. Ruth and Dana were a formidable pair—highly trained and quite ruthless former Israeli soldiers—and post facto worrying about them was a little uncalled for.

'I'll talk to Sanju so that we are all on the same page and see what to do next. It's his operation and we have to follow his lead. Meanwhile, let's eat something, rest a little and in the morning we'll do as Sanju plans.'

Gautam opened a bottle of wine for the ladies and himself, poured Yaakov a large whiskey—his drink of choice—and called Sanju.

'Syn-fucking-chronicity, Buddha,' exclaimed Sanju when he heard a detailed account of Gautam and his companions' adventures. 'It all seems to be coming together, G. Can't possibly be two different gangs at work here. Anyway, I'm sending Bhanu right away to meet up with your young Ben wherever he comes to rest. We'll give them each other's cell numbers, so they can coordinate. Tell him to simply note where these guys finally stop, then retreat and try and get some rest till Bhanu reaches him in about six hours. Then they can set up a watching brief on these characters. We've got another thread unravelling here which will connect us, hopefully, to the kidnappers tomorrow morning.'

Sanju told Gautam about their entrapment plan for Guddu in Gurugram the following morning.

'We'll get details of the operation from this Guddu fellow and take it from there tomorrow. Why don't you and Ruth just relax and let Dana get a cab from that village near you tomorrow morning and get to Kathgodam? I'll arrange for transport for her there and she can go relieve the Israeli boy, Ben, who can then go home and leave the business in my team's very competent hands. What say, Buddha?'

Gautam took a deep breath. 'Pandit is my problem, Sanju, and I intend to solve it once and for all. I have no intention of involving Ruth, but she's here and you know her.'

Ruth smiled and took a sip of wine. 'We—Ruth and I—will remain here for now and I'll ask Dana to go down and relieve Ben tomorrow and meet up with your man. We'll try and arrange some transport for her. Yaakov here has quite a few good friends and I'm sure he can rustle up something. We'll wait for whatever intelligence you all can get together tomorrow and plan a course of action. My concern is Pandit and his crowd, and if our targets are common, I'll coordinate with you to take them down. If they are different, I'll take down Pandit myself.'

'Fair enough, Buddha. Let's make plans tomorrow after getting some solid info. Could you ask Dana to call me, please?'

The cook served a simple meal—parathas, egg bhurji and gobhi aaloo—and immediately thereafter, Gautam spoke to Ben, while Yaakov, after a few phone calls, arranged for a taxi to pick up Dana early morning and take her to Kathgodam. Tired of the day's excitements, everyone decided to retire for the night.

Gautam held Ruth close once they were warmly ensconced under a large fluffy quilt—summer nights can be quite cool in the interior Himalayas.

'Glad you're back, even though things are a bit of a mess here,' said Gautam.

'I'm glad I'm back too. You get into too much trouble when I'm not around, my Colonel.'

Gautam laughed. 'And you are the peacemaker around here, my dear?'

Ruth sighed and shifted a little. 'Well, depends. For example, I can tell you are far too agitated for your own good, and need some stress release. So, if you will permit?'

Gautam kissed her gently. 'You must be tired from all your exertions—just sleep and we'll address the issue tomorrow.'

Ruth giggled. 'The issue, as far as I can make out, is growing in significance, my Colonel! And I'm never too tired when it comes to good deeds. Besides, my stress levels also need release. So will you stop talking and do some work please!'

By the time Ben left Bhimtal, still trailing the SUV, hunger pangs had become insistent. As he approached Kathgodam, he speed-dialed a number on his cell.

'Chotu Bhai, need your help, my friend,' he said, when the call was answered. 'I'll be reaching you in ten minutes or so and I'm in a great hurry, so please make two egg parathas and pack them up for me. I'll pick them up on the move. No, no, no time to stop, brother; in a big hurry. I'll see you aaram se on my way back. Just have the parathas ready, ok? I'm starving.'

Chhotu ran a bestselling paratha cart on the road in front of the railway station at Kathgodam. He was also one of Ben's pals in the town. Ben slowed down as he approached Chhotu's cart, fished out a hundred-rupees note from his pocket, grabbed the plastic bag that Chhotu's assistant held out, handed him the money and was on his way, without stopping his bike through the entire exchange. Traffic was heavy and he did not want to lose the SUV.

Chhotu shook his head at the mad antics of his foreigner friend who spoke idiomatic village Pahari, better than Chhotu himself who had become a townie after years in Kathgodam.

'Arre, don't worry about the change, Munnu. He'll be back soon enough. Here, start serving—people are waiting.'

Ben moved up closer to his target, confident of not being spotted given the mess of traffic on the Kathgodam-Haldwani roads.

By ten o'clock, Ashok's vehicle had crossed Haldwani and was on the road to Rudrapur. The tail end of the summer tourist season ensured a fair amount of traffic on the road and Ben fell back a bit and wolfed his parathas while they were still hot.

Pandit had reached the farm on the outskirts of Rudrapur during the day and was waiting impatiently for Ashok to arrive. The business with the Colonel had disturbed him more than he was prepared to acknowledge. He had not faced such determined opposition before and was finding it a little worrisome.

'The bastard is willing to go all the way,' he muttered to himself. 'Well, fine, so am I, as you will soon realize, motherfucker!'

A little after eleven, headlights coming down the kuchha road that led from the main metalled road to the farm announced Ashok's arrival. Pandit's farm was the last of four such farms served by the country road. The farmhouse was at the end of the road and insulated from the neighboring farmhouse by several fields of standing sugarcane.

When Ashok turned off the main road, Ben drove up slowly to the turnoff and halted, headlights switched off so as not to attract attention. The road wound through cane fields and once the Scorpio had disappeared round a distant curve, Ben followed slowly, without headlights, navigating by moonlight alone. The cautious approach paid off. Two kilometres down the road, as he rounded a bend, he saw the Scorpio about a hundred metres ahead, standing at a large iron gate leading to a walled enclosure within which a big house was visible. Bright lights illuminated the approach road to the gate and the porch of the farmhouse. The country track was bordered on both sides by huge old hardwood trees and Ben stopped in the shadow of one of the ancients and switched off the engine.

'Hope the fuckers didn't hear my engine noise over their growly diesel,' he muttered to himself as he fished out his binoculars and focused on the SUV ahead.

An elderly looking man opened the gates, the vehicle drove in and the gates were shut behind it.

'All right then, let's report back to HQ,' observed Ben and called Yaakov and Sanju.

Sanju asked for the GPS coordinates of the farmhouse and told Ben to leave immediately and try and get some rest wherever he could until Bhanu Bisht reached him.

'I've given your number to Bhanu and WhatsApped his to you. Just let him know your location and he will call when he approaches. Show him the place and then get back home. Thank you for everything—let my fellows do some work now.'

'Yes, sir,' responded Ben, turned his bike around and drove off to Rudrapur where he had a friend who would put him up for the night.

One look at Pandit and Ashok knew something was seriously wrong.

'You took your fucking time getting here, didn't you!' snarled Pandit when Ashok entered.

'Drove slowly, boss, just as you said,' replied Ashok softly and retreated into silence.

'And that fucking Pradeep isn't answering his fucking phone and neither is any other bastard on his team.'

Pandit took a deep breath and regained his composure.

'Get on the phone and don't get off till you have Pradeep on line, or one of his boys. And he'd better have a very good reason for not taking my calls.'

28

Bhanu Bisht reached Rudrapur and met Ben very early in the morning. The two resolved to visit the farmhouse after first light to get a clear idea of the layout, and if possible, of some of the occupants.

'It's a walled compound, boss,' Ben clarified, 'and a high wall at that. Can't see much.'

Bhanu grinned. 'I've a little toy in my Gypsy, Ben, that you might like. Our Israeli friends have given us two to check out in the field and my boss has given me one to play with. They are drones, a little bigger and more heavy duty than the ones film photographers commonly use these days. Mine has a good camera, a decent range and powerful batteries for a pretty good uptime. Plus, it can be guided very simply from a control console. Better than the best video game I've ever played, bro! We won't go too near them, just in case they are alert bastards. In any case, my remit is surveillance, so that is what we will do. We'll park about a kilometre away and launch the bird and see what's happening and report back to the boss.'

Ben laughed. 'I'm impressed. And I'm going to disobey orders to get back home right away. I want to see how this baby works.'

'Sure. Anyway, you can't leave me alone. You have to

wait for Dana to reach here and she's leaving in a couple of hours and will take at least six hours to reach. By then we should have some idea of the situation and the bosses can decide what to do, going forward. They are running some op in Gurugram this morning—picking up some guy involved in all this somehow—and should get some more data from him too. So we run our little toy and see what we see.'

'Great. You go and park on the main road close to the turnoff, just so they don't suddenly push off and leave us dangling. I'll organize some breakfast and bring it down as soon as my friend's shop opens. He makes the best samosas and bread pakoras in town and opens early to catch the truck traffic.'

Dana had requested for a cab at 5 a.m., but flexi-time being the order of the day with regard to early morning appointments, she left only at six from Gautam's estate. Gautam and Ruth joined Dana at the dining table with mugs of tea, while Bahadur dished up a substantial breakfast for her at five-thirty.

'Relax and enjoy, Ruth,' said Dana, as she was leaving. 'Leave the heavy lifting to us, Colonel. We have official resources, and they're good, so let us do the job.'

Gautam smiled. 'If I can persuade Ruth here to go back to Delhi—as befits a diplomat in this situation—I'll join you, Dana. I have business to sort out with Pandit.'

'If it is Pandit, Colonel. We don't really know, do we?'

'Has to be, in my view. Surveillance of the farm and Sanju's operation in Gurugram this morning should confirm it today. In which case, I'll talk to Sanju and take a call.'

Dana nodded, grinned at Ruth, got into the cab and left.

When Ben brought breakfast for Bhanu and himself, there was no sign of life on the road, barring an occasional commercial vehicle. Bhanu was parked fifty metres beyond the kuchha turnoff to Pandit's farm and the nearest structure was a dilapidated little shack located on the main road almost opposite the turnoff.

The two young men wolfed the hot fried snacks and then Bhanu unpacked his toy and got it ready to fly.

'Traffic will build up soon, boss,' observed Ben. 'We should get away from the road, say half a kilometre down the track, and then launch your bird away from curious eyes.'

'Yup,' concurred Bhanu. 'Let me get it ready and then we'll go down towards our target and launch. I'll be just ten minutes more. As long as I'm inside the vehicle, nobody can see anything much.'

Ten minutes later, Bhanu had his little drone ready and drove down the kuchha road leading to Pandit's farm with Ben following on his bike. They stopped about a kilometre down the path, invisible from the main highway, parked in the shadow of a huge old sheesham tree that had miraculously evaded the attentions of the timber mafia, and launched the bird.

A little careful manoeuvring brought the drone above the target farmhouse. Bhanu then programmed it to follow a circular flight path around the structure and they sat down to watch what the drone's cameras captured.

Nothing moved for about half an hour, then the front door opened and a tall man appeared, cellphone held to his ear and a large ceramic mug in the other hand. It was Pandit with his morning cup of tea talking to various people in Haldwani and Almora and finally, to Guddu in Gurugram. The drone took both stills and video clips, which were forwarded in near real time to the control and comm centre on Aurangzeb Lane.

Sanju got Pandit's photograph on his cellphone and sent it to Gautam, who promptly confirmed that it was indeed Pandit.

'It's confirmed, Fatso,' said an elated Sanju to a bleary eyed Datta sipping his first cup of coffee of the morning.

'G confirms it is Pandit at the farm that Bhanu and the Israeli boy are watching. Now if we can just get a glimpse of the French couple, everything ties up neatly. My boys are picking up the guy that's been communicating with the father of the kidnapped girl. Let's see what that yields. But things are coming together now.'

'So what's your plan?' asked Datta. 'If we are dealing with just one gang—this Pandit fellow's—and he is located at this farm, how do you plan to handle it? We'll have to keep Buddha in the loop. He's taken this Pandit thing personally.'

'Yes, he has, and that worries me too. Anyway, come along, let's brief Didi and her young gunwoman, and work out a plan.'

The young French couple in Pandit's custody had got fairly accustomed to their life in captivity. They were comfortably housed, well fed and unharmed. Pandit had even got them some books picked up from a newsstand at the railway station in Haldwani. Twice a day, they were allowed to walk around outdoors with an accompanying guard. In the mountains, their life had been quiet and rather pleasant. The trauma of the kidnapping and the fear and uncertainty about the future, they overcame by having a great deal of sex—they were young, healthy and believed themselves to be very much in love.

The forest fire and the sudden departure to the farm was a trifle distressing, especially since the weather was terrible as soon as they reached the plains. But youth has its advantages. They made sweaty love when they reached the farm and slept well despite the heat. In the morning, they asked for coffee and permission to go walkabout in the garden.

'Fuck, here they are, a young, white couple under obvious guard! We've got them!' said Bhanu, as the video of the couple walking out of the house and strolling about the rather neglected garden streamed on his monitor.

'Great. Let's get some back up and get this over with!' said Ben. 'Shouldn't take much doing.'

'Cool it, pal,' counselled Bhanu. 'Let the bosses take a call. There can't be too many people in there, given that only three vehicles are parked outside.'

Ben smiled and shrugged. 'No issues, boss. Just getting a little excited at the thought of some action other than vegetable farming and marketing.'

Shortly thereafter, Sanju confirmed the identities from the photographs he had in his possession.

29

Guddu, unlike most goons in Pandit's employ, could communicate in English and also make himself understood in what could be termed basic French and Italian. He had acquired these qualifications as a child in his home village of Khajuraho, vending artifacts to foreign tourists visiting the famous temples with their sculpture erotique. As a teenager, he had refined his language skills and certain other more dubious abilities as a guide to foreigners visiting Khajuraho. A fortuitous encounter with a lonely, no-longer-young, Italian lady brought him to Delhi and so began a career in crime focused on well-to-do foreign tourists who needed a very presentable and knowledgeable young man to show them round the medieval delights of the capital and its surroundings.

Pandit had met Guddu years ago when working as a tourist taxi driver for foreigners wanting to see the Himalayas, and he had established a sound, mutually profitable business relationship. Pandit planned carefully and paid well for efficient execution; Guddu was, therefore, very happy to work with him, despite Pandit being a rather frightening character.

At seven, as planned, Guddu was at the entrance to the metro station on MG Road, Gurugram to pick up the phone he had ordered. Within a minute he spotted Mannu, his contact in the 'mobile gang', approaching, accompanied by a middle-aged man he had not met before.

'Who's your friend?' enquired Guddu, as he smoothly exchanged an envelope of cash for a bag containing the phone he had asked for.

'This is Salim,' replied Mannu. 'He will meet all your requirements, Bhaiyya says.'

'Why, where are you going, brother? You know I like to do business with people I know well. Unless you want me to take my business elsewhere.'

'Don't be a fucking arse, Guddu. Bhaiyya is putting me on some new work and Salim here knows this business very well. Just check the fucking phone, I've got other work to do.'

'Very nice equipment, this,' observed Guddu after a comprehensive check of the device he had been given. 'Not very new, but quality stuff. Where did you get it?'

'Where I got it is none of your business,' interposed Salim—aka Sanju's Ismail. 'It is good till about midday, by which time the owner might realize it's missing and start making a ruckus. But you said you wanted a one-off phone, right? Just use it quickly and toss it. Let's go, Mannu, I don't like hanging around in public after a deal.'

Ismail/Salim had spoken in his usual deep low-pitched voice that made an immediate impression on listeners. Guddu, an acute observer of human beings by virtue of his trade, nodded acceptance. This Salim was not to be messed with, he concluded, and turned away after a perfunctory goodbye. Salim and Mannu moved off to where Salim's battered old Maruti was parked and Guddu entered the station. He paid no attention to the young woman with a backpack, who had preceded him on the escalator, or to the white-haired gentleman, who hurried up behind him, talking anxiously on a cellphone all the while.

Guddu's plan was simple enough. He would ride the metro for a few stations, get off and make his call, dump the phone, report to Pandit and head back home to West Gurugram and catch up on his sleep. He wasn't used to starting work at seven in the morning, but Pandit's instructions were clear.

Four stations down the way, he got off, as did the young woman with the backpack, who had been listening intently to something—presumably music—on her earphones. The white-haired gent, who was seated a few seats away from him, had been busily checking his mail on his cell. When Guddu rose to get off, the elderly gent followed suit and was talking softly on his phone when he emerged on the street close behind Guddu.

'He's off the train and walking down the road making a call. I'm ahead and Sharmaji is behind,' reported the young woman-with-backpack.

'Good, the boss is monitoring the phone and will tell us when we can pick him up. Stay loose. Not many people around, are there?' asked Ismail.

'No, not at this time,' replied the girl and Sharmaji muttered confirmation.

'Right then, I'll disconnect and wait for orders. Will call you.'

Sanju in his telecom centre in a dreary government building ostensibly occupied by a minor office of the Ministry of Culture, heard the conversation between Guddu and the kidnapped girl's father based in Paris.

The conversation was short and professional. Guddu

conveyed the message he had been asked to, disconnected, tossed the phone in an overflowing garbage bin, pulled out his personal phone and called Pandit to report.

Sanju called Ismail when Guddu's conversation ended.

'He's thrown away the phone, sir, and is making a call on another phone,' reported Ismail.

'Let him finish—probably reporting to his boss. As soon as he is done, pick him up and bring him to the safe house. I'll be there in twenty minutes.'

Ismail called his team.

'I'm moving up. Check that the coast is clear and grab him.'

Guddu reported compliance to Pandit, ended the call—Pandit was never one for small talk, and turned to walk back to the metro station, when someone bumped into him from behind.

'I have a gun against your back, Guddu,' said a hard, but distinctly feminine, voice, 'and my friend in front of you has another in that folded newspaper he's carrying. We need to talk to you and if you do as you are told we will not hurt you. Else, we'll drop you here in the gutter. Get into the car, now!'

Ismail's car rolled up as the lady finished and Sharmaji held Guddu's upper arm in an iron grip and propelled him into the rear seat.

In less than thirty seconds the car was on the move, Guddu and Sharmaji in the back, Ismail driving and Sheela, the lady operative, beside him. An oversize pair of dark glasses were thrust into Guddu's hands.

'Put these on, you won't see anything—the glass is opaque—because if you do, Guddu, we will have to kill you,' said Sharmaji in a soft, but utterly convincing, tone. 'Now, sit still and remain quiet. No questions, no talk.'

Guddu was not a hard guy. His weapons were usually charm and occasionally sex. Weapons and talk of being killed on the sidewalk sent him into panic.

'But…,' he began and stopped as something hard and metallic jabbed viciously into his side.

'I said, be quiet,' said Sharmaji in a harsh near whisper. 'Not another word!'

The rest of the journey to the Aurangzeb Lane safe house—thirty odd minutes—was completed in utter silence.

They led him to a room, tied his hands tightly behind his back and left him alone on a hard chair with a heavy black cotton hood over his head.

'He's not a toughie. Let him stew for an hour, then open him up quickly, Ismail. A touch of the taser on his arm and a threat to apply it to his balls should be enough, I think,' observed Sanju.

Ismail nodded. He was an expert interrogator and rarely used much actual force. 'Fear is always the key,' he would say in training programmes. 'And fear is in the mind, which is what you have to work on. You have to create that fear in the target's head and fan it to a point where it is overwhelming and ensures compliance. Of course, a fearful experience—a small taste—may be needed in case your target is really tough or you are in a great hurry. But some sensory deprivation for a while, along with the idea of what is going to happen, is usually enough.'

An hour in dark discomfort bordering on pain was enough to render Guddu compliant and eager to please.

'You are in deep shit, Guddu,' began Ismail, when he and Sanju entered the room where Guddu was incarcerated. 'And you have only one way of getting out of this in good health—do exactly as we say.'

'Sure, boss, anything, anything at all. Just tell me what you want, sirji. Please, just tell me and could you untie my hands, please, I'm hurting, I've got cramps, please sir.'

Ismail punched him hard in the solar plexus. 'Speak when you are told to, you son of a bitch,' he snarled.

'It's all right. Loosen his hands; as usual you've tied them too tight. And get him some water, while I tell him exactly what we want,' intervened Sanju.

Ismail left.

'My colleague is of the old school—break a few bones and everyone talks. But I think that will not be necessary, Guddu, what do you say? We have nothing against you, we just need everything you know about these people who have kidnapped this French couple. You see, we have recorded your conversation, so you can go to jail for twenty years without any effort on our part. And you won't do well in jail, Guddu, you're too pretty. If you cooperate, we give you a cash reward and set you free. We don't need you in court or anything—this matter is not going to any court, you get me? You need not worry about any reactions from your friends—they won't be around for very long. Now, before my colleague comes back and applies electric shock to your balls—we have a lovely little thing called a taser, a gun that can send electricity shooting through you and leave no mark at all—tell me you are ready to talk.'

Before Guddu could react, Ismail entered, slammed the door shut loudly, switched on a powerful portable lamp, pointed it at Guddu's face and then untied his hands and took off the hood.

'Here's your water,' he said and tossed a bottle to him. 'Drink up and start talking or else I apply my little electric gun to you. Maybe I should do that anyway, to give you a taste of what's in store if you act smart here, eh?'

Ismail reached across towards Guddu, holding a vicious looking Taser Pulse—a so-called 'less lethal' personal defense weapon.

Guddu started back in panic, almost dropping the water bottle. 'Oi, hold on, boss, please! I'll cooperate totally, totally, sirji, no problem! Just let me drink some water, sir, and I'll tell you everything I know, which is not much, but everything I know, I swear.'

Guddu talked for almost an hour with a pee break in the middle. They gave him some food, but that did not slow down the flow of words, and the intelligence gathered on Pandit was significant.

When it was evident that Guddu had run dry, Sanju got up to go.

'Now remember, Guddu, as discussed you will spend the next few days in the company of Salim sahib here,' he gestured towards Ismail, 'and his colleagues, doing exactly what they tell you. When your boss, what did you call him, Pandit, calls, you answer and do as he says. Once this is over, you are free as a bird with a bit of cash in your pocket as compensation. And remember, if ever you talk about any of this, Mr Salim will personally bury you in the Ghazipur landfill.'

Datta and the French officials had arrived and Sanju left to brief them, while Ismail and his team locked a hooded Guddu away in a small room in the servants' quarters beyond the back garden of the house.

'We've learnt a lot about Pandit today,'reported Sanju to Datta and the French agents. 'History and geography both, at least as much as Guddu knows. Operationally however, the best info is from the people in the field, as always. We'll hold on to Master Guddu till this is all over, then let him go.'

30

Bhim Singh Rautela had driven a truck for Pandit for many years during the early days when the latter had just begun his climb up the ladder of serious crime. For years Bhim Singh had ferried all sorts of contraband for Pandit and on two occasions taken severe beatings at the hands of rival smugglers while protecting his consignment from being hijacked. Pandit had tracked the hijackers, killed the leader and severely crippled two of his henchmen to provide living proof to the universe of the dangers of fucking with Pandit and his operations. Time passed, arthritis and alcohol took their toll and finally Bhim Singh was retired and placed as caretaker of one of the hideouts in the Berinag region. It was a comfortable sinecure for a widower whose three sons were married, working in far-away Delhi and who wanted no truck with a decrepit, near alcoholic, father.

When Pradeep left with Dana and Ruth, the old man stayed monitoring the forest fire racing down the hill. He did hear some odd minor explosions soon after the departure of the two vehicles—he was not unfamiliar with the sound of small arms fire—and a bigger explosion thereafter, but dismissed them as he was focused on the progress of the fire. Bhim Singh was just about ready to abandon his refuge when the clouds that had been gathering all afternoon opened up and the first of the pre-monsoon showers drenched the mountains. The forest fire was reduced to smoking embers; Bhim Singh heaved a sigh of relief and sought comfort in a half bottle of rum that Pradeep had kindly bestowed on him.

Very early morning, Pandit called Bhim Singh on the simple features phone he had been given and trained to use.

'What time did Pradeep leave yesterday?' asked Pandit. 'He was to call me and get here in the night, but he hasn't done that or taken my calls.'

'He left after talking to you, boss. I stayed back, and good I did, because it rained and the fire went out. The house is safe.'

'That's good, but Pradeep is not the sort to remain out of touch like this. It bothers me. He's also not stupid enough to drive off the road, but who knows, if a fuck up is possible, someone is sure to make it happen.'

Bhim Singh remembered the sounds he had heard last evening after Pradeep had left.

'I'll go down and check, boss. Just in case.'

'Yes, do that. Get a ride into Raiagar and ask around about any accidents in the area. I'll get Mintu to check with his contacts on the route to Almora and Haldwani. Let me know immediately if you learn anything.'

Bhim Singh walked down the hill to the main road. Close to where the mountain track met the black-top, he saw the aluminum guard rail broken and some debris on the road. He crossed the road, picked up some stuff, looked down the hillside and slowly charted a way to go down the steep-sided ravine to where the remains of an SUV were visible. He had a nasty feeling the vehicle was Pradeep's, but he had no intention of calling Pandit without personally confirming his suspicions. Giving the boss bad news was unpleasant, but giving him wrong info was positively dangerous. So Bhim Singh walked down the road to the point where he could lower himself on to a narrow pagdandi that would take him by a longish, gently sloping route to the bottom of the ravine.

An hour later, Bhim Singh was back on the road and dreading the call he had to make. He got his breath back and dialed Pandit.

'I can't find any trace of Pradeep. What news do you have?' asked Pandit immediately on taking his call.

'Er, boss, it is bad news. Just a little beyond where our road joins the main road, Pradeep's vehicle went off the road and into the khudd. It's very steep there, boss, you remember? I found some of their stuff—a keychain that Pradeep used to carry, a shoe of the pair he was wearing—on the edge of the road.

'I went down and checked their Scorpio. It had caught fire but the rain put it out. They are all dead, boss, Pradeep and his boys. Shot to death, boss, at least two of them; I couldn't get to the third. Pradeep and Harish had left with the two women in their Jeep and Sunny was following in the Scorpio. The Scorpio is in the khudd with the bodies and there is no sign of the Jeep and the women. I don't know how two women—they were white women, boss—could kill these boys and get away like this, but there it is. Unless somebody helped them, but how and who, I can't understand.'

Pandit was silent for a while. 'Did anyone see you checking out the Scorpio?'

'No, boss. Its early, there has been no traffic yet, but as soon as the taxis start, someone is going to stop and then the news will reach the authorities very fast.'

'All right. Get back to the house and stay there. Say nothing to anyone, nothing at all. You've seen nothing and you know nothing and nobody involved in this, understood?'

'Yes, boss,' replied Bhim Singh and trudged up the hill to his Himalayan refuge, thinking furiously. While he cooked a meal and consumed it, Bhim Singh came to a simple conclusion—it was dangerous to stay at the house and he had to get away. Whoever had killed Pradeep and his team may come back: the women knew the location. He packed his meagre belongings in a battered rucksack, dry rations in an old duffel, locked up the house and was soon deep in the woods in a small cave he had discovered years ago. It was a trifle damp, but a small fire made it quite cosy very quickly, and Bhim Singh took a well-deserved rest after all the recent excitement.

~

Pandit ended his call with Bhim Singh and stood immobile for a minute absorbing the information he had received and thinking through its implications. A foreign woman had taken Ashok and team out single handed—a woman who was driving into the mountains on a bike for a holiday; Pradeep had followed a single white woman in a fancy Jeep from Bhowali market, but when he hijacked the Jeep beyond Barechhina, there were two white women in it; in Israel, women were part of the Army in fighting positions; the Colonel had, early research had pointed out, a white woman as a girlfriend, who occasionally came up to his home in the mountains…

His gut told him very clearly that things had gone awry and it had something to do with that motherfucking

Colonel and his Israeli friends. The details were obviously unavailable, but evasive action had to be initiated until things became clearer. And Pandit trusted his gut.

He walked briskly into the living room yelling for Mintu, who appeared bleary eyed, a mug of tea in his hand; Mintu was not a morning person, but when Pandit yelled even Mintu—a senior thug—hurried.

'We move in half an hour. Get everyone ready, packed and fed, we have a long drive and we won't be stopping anywhere for some time. Quickly now, Mintu. Pradeep and his team are dead, shot close to the house on the main road and pushed off the road into the khudd. The women he had picked up have disappeared. Somebody—probably that fucking Colonel and his friends—is on to us to some extent. Whatever it is, we have to move fast and disappear for a while until the situation is clear and we have dealt with this son-of-a-bitch fauji. Business can wait, because it can't be done with this bastard somewhere in the shadows shoving his finger in wherever he feels like.'

Mintu turned to leave and then stopped. 'You think this Colonel got Jiten, boss? How, I don't know, but who else could have done that?'

'The news has spread, eh?' said Pandit. 'I don't know, but it's possible. We need time to be clear about what's happening and to take out this bugger. We'll do the exchange afterwards. Now get moving.'

31

'Something is not quite ok, bro,' muttered Ben, who was monitoring the feed from the drone, while Bhanu took a piss in the nearby field.

'Why, what's wrong?' asked Bhanu, zipping himself up and walking back to the vehicle.

'Everything was cool and everyone relaxed and chilling till ten seconds ago. This Pandit guy took a call, stood still for a while, walked inside and suddenly one of his guys rushed out looking very hassled and shoved the foreigners into the house.'

Bhanu took control of his little toy and brought it to hover above the front of the farmhouse. Soon a young man emerged, holding three backpacks that he dumped into one of the vehicles. Minutes later, another man appeared with more bags that he loaded into a second SUV.

'They are packing and moving. Shit, I must call the boss. And be ready to move, Ben, I don't want them to catch us here. Start up your bike; if they start driving, they will be here in minutes and we must be out on the main road ahead of them.'

Bhanu started his vehicle and called Sanju.

'Fuck, don't lose them, Bhanu,' said Sanju. 'And keep me informed.'

'Right, boss,' said Bhanu and disconnected.

'Now you're part of the team, Ben, no option,' said Bhanu. 'When they move, we'll get to the main road, you go left and stop somewhere close, preferably behind a tree or something, so they don't get a look at you; I'll turn right and stop. I'll need time to get my bird into its nest, so if they turn towards me you'll have to follow while I collect my toy; then we'll alternate. Ok?'

Ben grinned and mounted his bike and brought it next to Bhanu's Gypsy on the driver's side so as to get a look at the drone monitor.

'What if they split up, bro?' he asked.

'We follow the hostages, but we can't be spotted, Ben. I don't want the French couple to become fucking collateral damage.'

Ben nodded and the two watched the video feed in silence. In twenty minutes, the three SUVs were loaded and the passengers boarded. The hostages were with Mintu and his team. The elderly caretaker opened the gate and the convoy of three SUVs roared out, Ashok in the lead, Mintu with the hostages in the middle and Pandit in third position.

Bhanu and Ben left as soon as the gate was opened, drove fast to the main road and split as planned.

Pandit's convoy turned left on the main road and headed towards the hills at high speed. Ben who had parked behind a huge banyan tree, had stepped into the nearest field for a quick pee and was therefore invisible as the SUVs sped past. He let them proceed for a minute and then followed, keeping the last vehicle within eyeshot. Bhanu recalled his drone, packed it up hurriedly and followed, driving fast till he caught up with his partner and fell in behind him.

'We'll keep it this way for a while, Ben,' said Bhanu—they were communicating on cellphones—'and then you fall back and I will come up. We'll have to get closer when we get into Haldwani or else we may lose them.'

'Yes, and you'll have to be close to them—some of them may recognize me,' replied Ben. 'What about Dana?'

'I'll coordinate with her and our boss. Let's see which way these fellows go.'

32

Didi received a call from Paris soon after Guddu's conversation with the French was over, and called Datta.

'Paris just called, Mr Datta. The kidnappers have sent some instructions for the exchange.'

'Why don't you all come to the ops centre in an hour?' suggested Datta. 'Sanju and I will both be there and we have news too.'

Datta then called Sanju.

'Yeah,' replied Sanju. 'I heard the conversation. When can you join us at the ops centre?'

'Leaving now,' replied Datta and disconnected.

Datta reached the Aurangzeb Lane house within half an hour and the French agents soon after.

Didi began the briefing and Sanju and Datta listened silently.

'They are clever, these people,' she began. 'Their instructions are to get the money ready within two days and the exchange will be any time thereafter. Further instructions will follow.'

Didi looked at Datta and Sanju. 'How do you propose we proceed from here, gentlemen?'

'All yours, Sanju,' said Datta, gesturing to his friend to take over the proceedings.

'Clever indeed,' began Sanju. 'Minimum and precise instructions at each step. Incidentally, I was listening in to the conversation their man had with Paris and the fellow is in our custody here at this moment and we are letting him sweat for a while before opening him up. But all that apart, we have just got the location of the kidnapped couple. And that makes our planning much easier. They are in a farmhouse near Rudrapur very close to the mountains and about five hours drive from here. They are under surveillance by two of our people. At this point I do not want to plan any action, just move assets into position and wait for the details of the planned exchange. Since we have a fair amount of info on the kidnappers now, I'd rather wait, go through with the exchange, get the young couple out of harm's way and then take out the goons. I do not want to plan any kind of assault on the location for fear of collateral damage, Didi. So, I'm waiting for their detailed instructions for the exchange. Who will you send with the money when Pandit gives us instructions?'

'I will be the courier,' replied Didi.

'Cool. I suggest Ballu and Farah leave this evening and drive to Rudrapur—there are some nice hotels there. They will be close to the location and will wait there to hear what the kidnappers want and how we plan to deal with the affair. Dana should be joining up with Bhanu today—she's left from Gautam's place. Didi and our team here will wait for Pandit's instructions and we'll play the rest by ear. What do you say, Didi?'

'Dana, Bhanu, Gautam? Don't know these players, Sanjay.'

'Ah, yes. Dana and Bhanu are my colleagues; very efficient young people who will be backup for us.

Didi thought for a while and nodded. 'Congratulations. Though perhaps we could have been kept in the loop on this development, Sanjay. Just friendly cooperation, you know,' observed Didi.

Sanju grinned unrepentantly. 'That's exactly what I'm doing, Didi. All these are developments of the last twenty four hours or so.'

Didi nodded graciously 'Two teams for support is generous, Mr Datta, Sanjay. Executive decision making protocols, Sanjay?'

'All teams will be in constant communication—Ballu will distribute the equipment shortly—and strategy will be decided jointly; but, tactical field decisions will be mine as I will be accompanying you with my boys, Didi.'

'Thank you. And we are very grateful for everything you are doing.'

Balwinder distributed the telecom gear and demonstrated its working and then brought in the weaponry.

'I suggest you and Salim carry only handguns on your person,' said Sanju. 'The vehicle has some rather clever hiding places for a pair of submachine guns, just in case. Ballu and Farah can take along some heavier stuff. A sniper rifle may be useful in the hills and some flash and bang stuff, if you actually have to descend to battle, which I sincerely hope will not be necessary! Ballu, take along some extras—just in case—spare handguns, two submachine guns and ammo. Vests for everyone of course—we've got state of the art stuff now.'

Datta spoke up after the hardware had been distributed. 'The primary objective is to get the two young persons back safe and sound. We are not playing vengeance games here, right, Didi, despite all this talk of guns and so forth?'

Didi's response was immediate and emphatic. 'Absolutely, Mr Datta. My job is to ensure a safe exchange and I will not resort to any violence unless absolutely inescapable. I leave the law and order tasks to you all—it's your country.'

Datta nodded solemnly. 'Touché, Madame. Yes, we don't really approve of such lawlessness at all and will do everything in our power to bring these criminals to justice.'

Sanju watched this exchange with visible amusement. 'Now that everyone's said the correct, formal things, let's get this show on the road. Ballu load up your vehicle while Farah gets her stuff from the Embassy. Get your stuff and move in here, Didi, we have a reasonably comfortable room for you. Salim is based here and he and I will move with you as soon as we get the exchange details. And a cup of tea would be nice now, Salim, if your cook can manage it. Unless our guests prefer Nescafe?'

Didi shuddered dramatically. 'Please, Sanjay, not Nescafe. Black tea will be fine.'

Farah got up and moved to the door. 'I'll go get my bag,' she said with a slight smile. 'Anything to get away from your coffee, Salim.'

A quiet, self-satisfied atmosphere had descended upon the op centre. However, it was quickly shattered when Bhanu called to say that Pandit and team were leaving.

'Bloody hell! I hope the boys don't lose them. And just what fucking bee has got up Pandit's arse and provoked this sudden move?' exclaimed Sanju.

'If they are going to the hills, we'll have to change the disposition of our people,' observed Datta.

Sanju nodded, picked up his phone and dialed Dana, who was close to Almora in her taxi.

'Stop at Almora and see if your bike has been repaired.

If you're lucky and it has, then get hold of it and wait in Almora. We'll know where these people are going—or the general direction anyway, soon enough. In any case, get transport for yourself. Bhanu will make a few calls to get you something—he knows Almora very well. Check into the Shikhar—very convenient location—and await instructions. Things are very fluid at the moment so be prepared to move at short notice, Dana.'

'Right boss,' replied Dana. 'Do you think he's got news of the team we—Ruth and I—took out last night and is for some reason reacting to that?'

'Possible. Let me think on this. Let me know your status when you reach Almora. Bye.'

Sanju put down his phone and looked at Datta. 'Dana feels that Pandit may have got news of the team she and Ruth took out last night. And that has provoked this sudden move away from the farm. But, towards what? And why?'

Didi looked on, rather bewildered, while Datta nodded and went into a reverie that even the impatient Sanju did nothing to break.

In a while Datta shook his head and looked up at Sanju and said, 'You know, Sanju, we've not tried to put ourselves in Pandit's head and we should have. It is obvious that till now he was putting this hostage exchange business ahead of his business with Gautam. Until this morning, he was planning the exchange in a day or so; Gautam's transaction was obviously scheduled for later. But suddenly, he has lost the fellow that Gautam took out near Almora and now a three-man team is eliminated, out of the blue, in Buddha's area. I know all this is pretty tenuous, but what if he's decided that too many things are going wrong because he has left Buddha unattended, whereas he should have dealt with him first? What if that is what he is rushing to the mountains to do?'

'Bit speculative, but quite possible,' observed Sanju. 'Sorry, Didi, but detailed explanations will be forthcoming shortly. Two distinct threads seem to be converging and we have problems on our hands—and some calls to make.'

Sanju called Gautam and related the morning's events to him, including Datta's speculations.

'These guys are on the road to Haldwani, as per Bhanu. Once they get into the hills, we shall be clear about their general direction. They may have some other fucking hideout. Who knows? Anyway, you take all necessary precautions. Dana is at Almora until we know what the fuck's actually happening and I'll have some plans activated in a couple of hours. I'll keep you updated on Pandit's movements—you can also talk to Ben directly. And get that other Israeli boy on active duty, don't let him go back home yet. We'll talk in a while.'

Sanju looked at Datta, 'Didi and I with our teams should all move ASAP towards the hills. The hostages are moving with Pandit and his boys, and so we move too in pursuit. He obviously does not want the exchange right away. But regardless we shall be very close to him when he stops moving and will work out what to do then. Can't just sit here and wait for Pandit to call. Too many unknowns emerging now.'

Datta nodded agreement. 'Yes, too many uncertainties in the picture. You guys move and keep in touch with Gautam. Wrap it up as you see best Sanju, and soon.'

33

Gautam turned to Yaakov and Ruth when Sanju's call ended.

'Sorry folks, we have a new problem. It appears that Pandit and gang have suddenly abandoned the farm and are heading towards the hills at speed. Sanju has Ben and Bhanu following them and will keep us posted about their movements. However, Datta has had one of his famous "gut reactions" and suspects that Pandit has heard about his missing team that you girls took out of play, Ruth, and has decided that we here constitute a problem that has to be tackled first. So, we have to be ready for aggressive action very soon.'

'Cool,' responded Yaakov. 'And how do you plan to deal with him, Colonel? I'm sure you have a plan. Also, I must inform Deb—they would like to participate, I believe.'

'I'm not sure about that, Yaakov. Why should they get involved—you and Ben are help enough.'

Yaakov laughed. 'You don't know Deb, Colonel. She's the complete warrior—the rest of us are just trained soldiers, as we had no option. At heart, Reuben is a healer and Ben and I are farmers. Anyway, I have to inform her that an attack appears imminent and let her take a call on what they want to do. I'm, of course, here, at your disposal.'

Gautam nodded and Yaakov stepped outside to try and get better connectivity on his cellphone.

Gautam turned to Ruth and said, 'You've been very quiet for very long; and that worries me. C'mon say something.'

Ruth smiled. 'I'm waiting for you to tell me to leave for Delhi—get back to work and let you get on with business here, my Colonel. Go on, say it and clear your conscience.'

Gautam smiled back ruefully. 'It's the only sensible thing to do, Ruth. As an Israeli diplomat you cannot be found participating in local battles. It will have all sorts of repercussions.'

Ruth nodded solemnly. 'It will also keep me out of harm's way. I guess I should go home and brush up on my baking techniques or something, eh, Gautam? And leave you and Yaakov to face the deadly Pandit all on your own. We Jewish women are famous for our breads and for running away from battle, especially when our men are facing grave danger from nasty enemies, right?'

Gautam shook his head. 'For the last time, please, drive down to Delhi, Ruth. We are quite capable of dealing with this gang without involving diplomats and inviting future complications.'

Ruth grinned at Gautam. 'Why waste time, my Colonel? The evil ones are speeding towards us and we are sitting here nattering away about silly issues. Let's start preparations. It won't do to underestimate this crowd.'

Gautam raised his hands in surrender and called for Sher Bahadur, his cook, who entered just as Yaakov returned after completing his call.

Gautam looked questioningly at Yaakov, who reported that Deborah and Reuben would move within the hour and would be at Gautam's place by early afternoon.

'Ask them to call before approaching the place. I don't want them to run up against Pandit and Co. unprepared.'

Yaakov nodded. 'Will do in a couple of hours when they will have better connectivity facing us across the valley.'

'Right. Now come with me and let's get all the equipment sorted out.'

Gautam led the way to a small room that appeared to be a store house for unwanted junk, shifted a dusty wooden almirah full of old books aside and revealed a walk-in cupboard like structure which was, in fact, a steel weapons safe containing a small, but very lethal armoury of small arms, ammunition and related warlike material.

'Wow, this is heavy stuff!' observed Ruth and Yaakov nodded agreement.

'The Colonel is well prepared, Ruth. So how do we do this boss?'

'Let's get the haversacks, they are in that cupboard,' said Gautam pointing at another dusty steel almirah across the room.

'Ok, now everyone gets basic armament—a handgun and three mags, spare ammo and a combat knife. All firearms are 9mm. Everyone gets a vest—the best US military issue and no shortage—and we carry some for our friends in the field; Sanju will bring equipment for his team. There is just one sniper rifle and three submachine guns and the rifle Yaakov took off Pandit's man, though that's not 9mm. Besides, I don't think we're going to need all this stuff. Bring it all out into the drawing room and let's distribute it anyway.'

'How come they gave you so much hardware, Gautam?' asked Ruth. 'Not quite typical government behaviour…'

Gautam nodded agreement. 'True. But when Bhima's

dope factory had to be taken down, we needed more than just handguns, and later, when Mr Mo had to be dealt with, equipment for these guys,' Gautam gestured towards Yaakov, 'had to be provided and the stock just built up. In fact, I returned some stuff, but old Ayengar was a far-sighted guy. He insisted I keep a lot of it, just in case! The paperwork must have been a nightmare.'

34

Pandit's convoy roared up the kuchha road from the farmhouse in a cloud of dust. At the junction where it met the tarred main road, with much screeching of breaks and roaring acceleration of diesel mills, the convoy turned east and drove towards the hills. Once beyond the crowded and potholed Rudrapur roads and on the forest road to Haldwani, they picked up speed. Pandit spoke to Guddu, incarcerated in Sanju's safe house, instructed him to advice Paris about the delay in the hostage exchange and let slip the fact that he, Pandit, had some urgent business to attend to. He then turned to young Alok.

'In Haldwani, don't go straight through—drive around those fucking narrow gullies a little—I want to see if anyone's following us'

'But, boss…'

'And don't use your brains, arsehole,' snarled Pandit. 'Just do as you are told. There was a newish SUV parked on the main road close to our kachhi sadak from the farm and a motorcycle behind that big banyan tree. Now it could be nothing at all, but I'm allergic to motorcycles, so just wander around Haldwani a bit, slowly, and we'll see what we will see.'

Alok nodded and picked up speed.

When Pandit had called Guddu for the second time, he—Guddu—was in the tender loving care of Ismail and team in the ops centre on Aurangazeb Lane and Sanju, Datta and the French team were in the drawing room having just learnt from Bhanu and Ben that Pandit was leaving the farm and heading towards the hills.

Ismail conveyed Pandit's message to postpone the exchange and added the nugget that Pandit had let slip that he had important business to attend to. This more or less confirmed Datta's suspicion that Pandit had decided to dispose of Gautam before doing anything else.

Sanju called Gautam immediately. 'Pandit just called his fellow who's in our care, Buddha. Told him to advise Paris that the hostage exchange will be delayed for a few days. And then he let slip to his boy that he had some urgent business to attend to. So Datta appears to have been right—he's apparently coming for you. I'll leave with the French agents and my boys within an hour—we're loading up as we talk—but I'll be several hours behind Pandit, unless he stops en route. Anyway, let's get moving from here and we'll talk. You are prepared for whatever this fucker may be planning?'

'Just distributing the hardware; then I will outline my basic plan, have lunch and take up positions. Don't worry, Sanju, and don't drive too fast!'

'Jesus, Buddha, you don't ever change!' Sanju exclaimed and disconnected.

'Alright, folks,' announced Sanju to the others. 'We move ASAP, so let's get to it. Didi, get your stuff from the Embassy right away. Ballu will load up here and we'll be waiting for you—we leave in an hour, as you heard me tell my friend on the phone. I suggest Didi and Farah ride with

Ballu and me to begin with. I can brief you folks on the other threads of this operation, and Salim drives the other vehicle. At Gajaraula, we will take a comfort break. Our comms centre will be running 24/7 here and Datta will be on call in case we need anything.'

As they approached Haldwani, Bhanu moved up a little closer to Pandit's vehicles. The traffic on the road had picked up and there were plenty of trucks to provide cover. Ben kept a safe distance behind Bhanu.

'Hey, they are not taking the straight route out of the town, Ben,' reported Bhanu when Pandit's convoy turned into the residential part of the town and its narrow streets, instead of going right through the main bazaar and out to Kathgodam.

'Maybe they want to stop somewhere or they are checking for tails,' replied Ben.

Bhanu laughed. 'I was born and brought up here, man. I know every damn lane in this town. But I tell you what, you go through to Kathgodam and hang around opposite the railway station and I'll keep you updated on their movement. If they fuck around the town and then go up towards the hills, I'll tell you and you can tail from the front. If they are being clever and decide to go off in any other direction, I'll call you to catch up. So go through and wait near the station.'

'Good idea. Just don't lose them pal, that's all,' replied Ben, and when Pandit, with Bhanu in tow, turned into the town, he worked his way through the bazaar traffic, drove to the Kathgodam station and stopped at his friend's cart for a cup of tea.

Bhanu was clever and as knowledgeable about Haldwani as he claimed to be. Alok's twists and turns to identify any followers yielded no results as Bhanu was careful to take parallel lanes where possible instead of following Alok directly into every residential colony that he dived into. But then the inevitable happened. On one such parallel lane, Bhanu's way was blocked by a broken down mini truck and he lost track of Pandit's convoy.

'Listen, I've lost them Ben,' he reported. 'But from the point where I lost them they can either go towards Kathgodam or get out of town in the opposite direction. Since you are at the station keep a look out for them and let me know if they come that way. If I spot them on the Kaladhungi route, I'll call you, ok?'

'Sure, boss,' said Ben resignedly and concentrated on watching the approaching traffic from Haldwani side while maintaining an idle conversation with his friend, Chhotu, the paratha and samosa vendor.

Though traffic was sparse, there was a small crowd around Chhotu's cart—his regulars getting an early high-carb, deep fried breakfast before the day's work started. Ben had parked his bike behind the cart so as not to disrupt Chhotu's customer flow and sat straddling the bike, sipping tea and keeping an eye out for Pandit's vehicles.

As they turned onto the main road leading to the hills via Kathgodam, Pandit suddenly said, 'Stop and pick up some food at the station, I'm hungry.'

'Yes, boss, the bread pakoras and samosas at Chhotu's are excellent—hot and fresh at this time,' replied Alok, happy at the thought of breakfast before what promised to be a long, hard day's driving in the mountains.

'Good,' replied Pandit. 'Park a little ahead—I don't

want to attract the attention of all the fucking idlers around the station, and run back and get some stuff. I'll tell the others.'

Pandit conveyed his instructions to his team and as they roared past Chhotu's cart, Ben started his bike and made to follow. As he pulled into the street, he saw Pandit's convoy stop fifty yards down the road.

'Fuck!' Ben muttered to himself and spotting a narrow lane taking off from the main road, quickly drove into it and stopped where the lane took a turn that hid him from the road. Ben parked and made his way back carefully, just in time to see Alok and two others trotting down towards Chhotu's cart.

The lane offered no concealment, but a tiny hole-in-the-wall shop selling paan-bidi-cigarette-mineral water and cold drinks had just opened for business on the main road. Ben took off his helmet, fished a cap out of his pocket and, helmet in hand, cap on head, walked over to the shop and began a slow and mildly argumentative process of cigarette and bottled water purchase.

Ben had concluded his transaction, packed his purchases in a plastic carry bag and was amiably discussing the emerging political situation at the national level, when Pandit's trio started back with laden paper bags.

And then two of the Pandit trio decided to stock up on cigarettes. Fortunately, it was not Alok who crossed the street. Alok didn't smoke and also wanted to get back quickly as he didn't want to be the focus of Pandit's well known impatience.

As the duo approached the shop, Ben hurriedly concluded the conversation and turned away towards the lane where his bike was parked.

The shopkeeper was a chatty soul and as Pandit's men bought cigarettes, he nattered away in a friendly fashion.

'Today's going to be a good day, folks,' he said optimistically. 'I've started getting customers as soon as I opened. That foreigner came in just before you; amazing fellow—speaks as good Pahari as I do—in fact hard-core village dialect that I've almost forgotten, living here in town for so many years. Must be one of those Israelis here for charas and ganja after their army stint. Army service is compulsory there, I understand, and after that they all come here or go to Himachal, and stay stoned for years until they run out of money. Here you go, your change. Are you sure you don't want to carry some water? The naulas are all drying up despite the pre-monsoons having started. No? Ok then, have a good journey.'

A peremptory toot from Pandit's SUV nudged the boys into jogging hurriedly back to their vehicles and moving off. It was only when they were well on their way climbing up the mountain on the Bhimtal road that the penny dropped and one of the goons who was riding with Mintu thought to relate the details of the cigarettewalla's conversation.

Mintu Mobile was both quick on the uptake and quick to react. As Pandit's senior-most lieutenant, he was also less in awe of him than the rest. He thought for a while, then called Pandit and related the details to him. 'It may mean nothing at all, boss, just another foreigner buying cigarettes in the morning, but I think we should take some precautions.'

Pandit fought back a rising tide of fury at the malign workings of fate and took a quick decision. 'Yes, we must and it's good you saw the need for it. Everyone keep a lookout for any bike following us and take the Ramgarh road from Bhowali—a nice and quiet road for our work. If indeed we are being followed by a biker, we will take him out somewhere beyond the turnoff for Mukteshwar. Now get everyone alert and watching. We should have confirmation by the time we are around Ramgarh.'

35

'So, what's the plan?' asked Ruth, once all the war-like equipment had been distributed and put away in backpacks. Sher Bahadur was busy cooking and Gautam had led Ruth and Yaakov out to the verandah.

'Since I moved in here, Sher Bahadur and I have been working to build hideouts on the ridge above and some defensive positions on the property and the bit of forest below, between my land and the main road. We started it as a lark and it continued as a slightly neurotic and insecure activity—you know, ex-servicemen still playing soldier! While lunch and our battlefield rations of parathas and aachar get done, I'll take you around and show you the spots. Let's do the ridge first. Basically, we found a natural cave, a small erosion in a rocky cliff face, and deepened and fixed it up as temporary quarters in case the house had to be abandoned for tactical reasons. A near impenetrable thicket of rhododendron extending right up to the cliff face conceals it completely. We've made access pathways—one is actually a crawlway—that are very hard to spot. Then, we have a couple of sniper positions overlooking the property and an actual machan that I challenge anyone to spot from the ground or from anywhere else, for that matter. I spent a night there when a female leopard had selected the ridge as a birthing hide, hoping to catch her on camera. But she was too savvy—I caught just one fleeting glimpse, once early morning, but nothing more.'

The threesome toured the ridge and all the secret places therein and returned for an early lunch. Gautam then walked them quickly around the property and showed them the concealed rifle pits there and between the property and the main road.

As Yaakov got ready to set off and intercept his colleagues from Tinauli, Gautam said, 'Remember, do not come up to the property before talking to me. We have three options here. If Pandit is stupid enough to come charging up in broad daylight, complete with hostages in tow, we'll deal with him here. However, I'm sure he will do no such thing. The second option is, he dumps the hostages at some safe house—the cottage where Ruth and Dana were held, for example, and then comes for us after dark. In that case, we can either ambush him on the road—I have selected an excellent site that is half an hour out of Raiagar towards us—or we can tackle him while he is still at his safe house. The last is the best option. I have no wish to make my home a battle zone and would much rather take it to them—makes disposal problems much easier, too. Anyway, everything is fluid at present, so we'll see what develops and act accordingly. We have to keep things flexible, Yaakov, so keep in touch and we'll take it as it comes. Leave your bike here—no point announcing to the village that you are around by parking the bike there.'

'Wow. You do have a detailed plan of action, my Colonel,' said Ruth with a laugh and Gautam smiled back.

'In a fluid situation, one remains fluid, right, Major?' he replied. 'Come on, let's talk to Ben and Bhanu and Sanju.

Communication lines are critical in such fast-changing scenarios.'

Ruth grinned, snapped off a smart salute and they went indoors.

~

A broken down truck and a small landslide—thanks to the recent pre-monsoon showers—had created a traffic jam on the Bhimtal road and Pandit's convoy stopped at the tail end of a kilometre-long line of vehicles inching their way forward. Ben caught a glimpse of the jam from a wide curve, stopped well before he would have bumped into Pandit's vehicles, and called Bhanu. 'If you haven't started on the Bhimtal road, I suggest you take the old Gethia-Bhowali Sanatorium road and stop at Bhowali near the bridge that leads to Ramgarh. We have to come that way, unless they turn off somewhere en route. But for that they don't have many options. I'll let you know if they do and you catch up as best as you can.'

Bhanu laughed. 'I'm just leaving Kathgodam and I'll take the old Nainital road. Let me know your progress.'

~

Sanju and his team accompanied by the French agents made good time on the highway towards Moradabad.

Sanju's briefing about Gautam and his role in the affairs at hand was very brief, cryptic even.

'We have a close friend, an ex army-man, we call him Buddha or G, who has retired to a small and rather lovely property in the interior Kumaon to grow potatoes and stuff. Recently, he reported a serious attempt to hijack his property; some local goons threatened him with dire consequences if he didn't agree to sell his property to them at some silly price. He's a tough guy, our G, and he refused. We were thinking of how to deal with this when your young lady tourist got herself kidnapped in the same area. Organized crime of this sort is, or at least was, rare in the mountains, so we wondered if the same set of people could be behind both things. Now it is established that the same gang is behind both events, so we, er, sort out two problems with one stroke, so to speak.'

'Your friend won't be the same Special Forces Colonel who helped sort out—rather terminally, we are told—some drug related issues for you recently?' asked Didi.

Sanju raised his eyebrows, but said nothing.

'Oh, come on, we would check up on you lot when we are sent on such an important mission. Wouldn't you have done the same if you were told to work with some unknown set of foreigners on a sensitive op like this one?' protested Didi.

Sanju grinned and replied, 'Of course, I would have. And I'm impressed with your sources. The Yanks have obviously been talking, or the Israelis, who too sometimes leak when it suits them. Anyway, yes, it is the same person and no more details please. He has some help with him and I'll brief you further once we have a clearer idea about where this Pandit fellow is headed with your hostages. We suspect he's headed to deal with G, who's been hurting him a good deal in the past few days. But let's see; we'll have a detailed briefing when any sort of action is planned. For now, we are too far off from the scene.'

At Gajaraula, Didi shifted to Salim's vehicle—its

useful to be familiar with one's collaborators in such tricky situations—and they sped on via the Moradabad-Bazpur-Haldwani route towards Kathgodam and the mountains.

Bhanu reached Bhowali first and parked in a clutter of cars near the bridge that led to Ramgarh. A fruit stall was displaying the last of the local seasonal fruit, Kaphal, and Bhanu stood there, examining it in detail and negotiating price till he saw Pandit's convoy of dusty SUVs barreling down the road aggressively. Finalizing his purchase, he called Ben.

'They are here and—wait a minute—yes, they are turning towards Ramgarh. I'll wait a while, eat some kaphal—which are super by the way—and then get after them. You hang back. Where exactly are you?'

'Just coming down the hill from the pass, will be there in ten minutes.'

'Ok. I'll move in five and you wait another five and follow. I'll inform Sanju and Colonel Shukla.'

On the Bhowali-Ramgarh-Almora road, Pandit and team kept a close watch on the traffic behind them.

'Can't see anybody following us, boss,' Mintu reported on the cell. 'Just the usual tourist traffic—one SUV, two Maruti Alto taxis and one fancy sedan—probably a BMW, but I'm not sure. Not able to get a clear look. All probably on their way to Mukteshwar.'

Pandit grunted assent. 'All of New Delhi's South

Extension has a holiday home in Mukteshwar. But I'm glad. They have raised the price of land and the value of properties like the Colonel's no end. But tell me, Mintu, why is that SUV not overtaking us? It's the most powerful vehicle on the road at present and it's letting those piddly Marutis overtake it.'

'Narrow road, boss. Altos are more agile and taxi drivers more reckless.'

'Hmm,' replied Pandit, unconvinced. 'Keep watching, don't sleep off. We'll go to the big house in Almora—I want to pick up some heavy equipment—and I've told Pandeji to make some food. We'll eat quickly and move on—I want to deposit these foreigners with Bhim Singh at the cottage, get some rest and go pay the Colonel a visit in the late hours. This tamasha ends tonight.'

'Yes, boss,' replied Mintu as Pandit disconnected.

'Let's hope your simple plans survive first contact with the enemy, Gautam,' observed Ruth, as they sat in the verandah with cups of hot tea.

Gautam laughed. 'We know they never do, but we have to start somewhere and then improvise to match developments.'

Ruth smiled and stretched. 'You do have a bit of paradise here, don't you, Gautam? The high Himalayas almost at your doorstep, oak forest all around you, summer flowers in your garden, a cool breeze blowing and that darned bird—Himalayan thrush, is it—that insists on singing to you every time you come out of the house!'

Gautam laughed. 'Don't tell me you're jealous of my little friend, Ruth?'

Ruth laughed in response. 'I'm not jealous of her, my Colonel. I quite approve of her taste in men! Anyway, since it's such a lovely day, I think I'll have me a short nap.'

Ruth was asleep in the armchair within minutes. Beside her, Gautam sat, breathing slow and deep, his mind growing increasingly quiet.

He remembered his archery sensei's words:

'You train and train and train so when the time comes you get out of the way and IT shoots.'

Gautam had simply nodded while the Master had continued, 'At least you don't ask, like my Western students, what IT is.'

The old man laughed briefly. 'They are puzzled when I say I can't describe IT but they will know IT when they encounter IT.' He laughed again. 'Many leave at that point—they cannot deal with unexplained mysteries.'

~

As Pandit's convoy, followed by Bhanu and Ben, joined the main Khairna road to Almora and began the ascent to the town, Bhanu called Dana. She had reached Almora some time ago and found her bike repaired and ready to go.

'We'll be there soon, what are you planning?'

'I'll drive down to where the old toll house was and hide myself in one of the souvenir shops there—there are so many of them now—and follow them when they go through. You guys hang back—I'll brief you as we go along.'

'Cool. Keep in touch, Dana,' said Bhanu and informed Ben, and then Sanju and Gautam, on a conference call which miraculously went through.

'Let me know when they and you guys leave Almora.

Everything will now depend on where they are headed. We don't know all their hideouts or what that Pandit fellow has planned,' said Gautam. 'If they come our way now, I plan to take them out right here. We'll talk when things are clearer, but cellphone connectivity gets a little iffy as you move into the interior, although it's generally good all over the hills. So, just in case we get cut off, stay back from them when—and if—they turn from Raiagar towards my place. Ruth and I will be in position well before they reach there and for that you must let me know when they turn off from Barechhina towards Raiagar. Connectivity is good there. And don't fret if you can't get through, I'll compute driving times from Almora and start moving approximately when I expect them to pass 'Chhina.'

Sanju took an impatient breath. 'For fuck's sake, Buddha, I know you've worked it all out—dotted every t, crossed every i—and I am still too far from the action!'

Gautam laughed. 'Stop being so damned impatient, Sanju. They will probably come only at night, so you may well be here for the fun. Just drive carefully—the pre-monsoons may play havoc with some of our roads, you know that.'

'Yes, granny, I'll be careful and not talk to any strangers either. Bye for now.'

36

Pandit's party took the lower road parallel to the old mall road and Dana followed minutes later. When Pandit's convoy stopped at a big house a couple of kilometres down the road, Dana too stopped, well short. Then, when the men had entered the house, she drove past without stopping, parked when out of sight of the house and walked back to a convenient restaurant from where the SUVs were visible. She occupied a table, ordered coffee and an omelette, picked up a newspaper from an adjoining table and took up a watching position. She informed Bhanu of the current status and he parked near the old toll house on the outskirts of town and waited for Ben.

When Ben caught up they spoke to Dana. 'I suggest Bhanu and I go through on the Mall road, grab a bite and get to the other end where Pandit and company will come out when they leave. If they do something weird like going back the way they came, you follow them, Dana, and let us know, and we'll hurry back—its no great distance,' said Ben.

'Sure, sounds sensible,' replied Dana, disconnected and addressed the surprisingly well-made meal presented to her.

An hour and three cups of coffee later, Dana saw the SUVs start up and move out. She paid her bill, called

Bhanu and waited till Pandit and party were out of sight before following.

'They are coming towards you, boys. I'm a few minutes behind.'

'Great, we're ready to move; me first, then you join in, Dana, and Ben last, as some of them may recognize him, if they are locals. These firangis are notorious drunks and womanizers in this part of the world!'

Dana heard Ben laugh in the background, as she started her bike.

'On my way, boys,' said Dana and accelerated after Pandit's convoy.

Ben informed Gautam and Sanju, while Bhanu kept a look out for the SUVs. As soon as he spotted them, he moved on ahead towards the Barechhina-Pithoragarh road intending to tail from the front. Ben hung back out of sight until Pandit's vehicles went through, followed in a few minutes by Dana, and then brought up the rear.

'All right, they have left Almora with our three teammates in tow,' announced Gautam to Ruth after taking Ben's call. 'It will take them three hours to reach Raiagar and another hour and a half to get to us, if they are coming here. Get some more rest, Major, plenty of time.'

Ruth sketched him a salute. 'A small suggestion, sir, simply for operational efficiency. If we retire to your room for a while and get into bed, we may be better prepared for what's coming. You know, be stress free and fully "mindful" for combat. Just a suggestion, of course, sir, for consideration of the respected commanding officer.'

Gautam looked quietly at her, then smiled. 'Excellent idea, Major, approved,' he said, got up, held out his hand and led her to the bedroom.

Half an hour later, they had a hot shower together, dressed and returned to the verandah.

'That was rather intense, wasn't it?' observed Ruth.

'Hmm,' was Gautam's only reaction.

'I need some hot, sweet tea,' said Ruth getting up. 'I'll make some for you, too, if you smile and say something other than hmmm.'

Gautam smiled and said, 'Please, lots of tea, while I check where Yaakov and the Tinauli gang are.'

Yaakov answered his cellphone immediately. 'We're about twenty minutes out, Colonel,' he said. 'Deb has been doing a forced march and is making us almost run up the damned hill—says we've gone soft!'

Gautam laughed. 'Good. Come up to the house and we'll talk. We can only finalize plans once we know which way they go from Raiagar.'

'Sure, boss. See you in a while.'

'We seem to have a woman on a motorbike behind us, boss, another bike way behind, no SUV that I can see,' Mintu reported to Pandit.

Pandit grunted. 'It was a woman on a bike who took Ashok and his boys out, Mintu; but for now, keep moving. At Barechhina, tell Ashok to fall back, you take the lead and I'll be in the middle. Ashok can try and check if the woman behind is, by any chance, his old friend. If it is, he should simply let her follow us to the cottage. I will deal with her there. I need to talk to her to clarify matters. Too many fucking unknowns here.'

Mintu conveyed Pandit's instructions to Ashok on call and sat back. He was getting worried—Pandit was not his usual self and that was disturbing. Tangling with this colonel was turning out to be expensive and who was this mystery woman anyway?

37

'Wow, the Himalayas at last!' exclaimed Farah on first sighting the mountains as they approached Haldwani.

'Wait till your first glimpse of the snows—if you get one in this weather. It's truly mind boggling,' replied Sanju.

'I can imagine: Nanda Devi, Trishul and all the others in a row. I plan to go trekking there one day.'

'You are well informed.'

'Yes, I trek in my free time, of which I have too little unfortunately. But India and Nepal are my next targets.'

'Sounds ominous, but do let us know, we should be able to help. Now, anybody need a comfort break or shall we push on up the hill and stop at Mehragaon? There's a very nice café by the roadside with clean loos and excellent food. We'll pack some snacks and keep moving.'

'Sounds great,' replied Farah and the team swept through Haldwani-Kathgodam into the mountains.

Sanju was getting increasingly restless. Pandit and team would be approaching Raiagar in about an hour's time and the final scenario for a confrontation would emerge thereafter. He called Gautam, who answered on the first ring.

'Getting jittery, Sanju!' was Gautam's opening greeting. 'Relax, we are having tea and waiting for word from Ben and Bhanu. All set to receive our friends, if they come now.'

Sanju laughed. 'Locked and loaded for the Gunfight at the Colonel's Corral, eh Buddha? Let's hope it doesn't come to that.'

'I don't think so, Sanju, but we'll know soon enough. We'll move into position if they turn this way. You take it easy and keep in touch.'

Gautam disconnected and put the phone down.

'You're very quiet, Ruth, what's up?'

Ruth shook her head. 'Just soaking in the ambience of this place. The quiet does creep into one, even when a battle is imminent.'

'Yes it does, in fact, especially when battle is imminent; especially for seasoned old soldiers, isn't it?'

'Speak for yourself, old man,' said Ruth with a laugh and turned to look at the chiaroscuro of the mountainscape stretching away towards the horizon.

The road to Raiagar from Barechhina winds down through a forested hillside to a river and then climbs up quite steeply. It took Ashok some time and the assistance of a good pair of binoculars to identify Dana.

'It's the same woman we encountered earlier, boss,' he reported to Pandit. 'We had knocked her off the road, but she seems to have survived and got her bike repaired somehow.'

'Sure? With a helmet on, all you have to recognize her by are her tits?'

'Yes boss, nice tits, but the bike is more easily recognizable. It's her boss, the same bitch, no doubt.'

'Ok. Do nothing and keep up with us. I want her to follow us to the cottage where we can have a chat. Maybe she's spotted you on the road and simply wants to kick your arse one more time. Anyway, I need to know more, so just let her come.'

Pandit called old Bhim Singh, who somehow had phone connectivity even in his cave. 'We will be at the cottage in about two hours. Get food ready for nine people.'

Bhanu stopped at Raiagar, walked over to a chai shop, ordered a glass of the local brew, which he had no intentions of drinking, and called Gautam.

'I'm at the junction, Colonel, waiting for Pandit and friends to catch up. Any instructions?'

'Just let me know which way they go and continue to follow at a safe distance. If they are going to a safe house, I want them to feel very safe and secure—no fears of followers or anything. If they go off road, do not follow, just mark the takeoff point and stand off and watch it such that you can't be spotted if they send someone back to stand guard. Just keep in touch so there's no confusion when we make an action plan.'

'Right, sir,' replied Bhanu, disconnected, and then in quick succession called Sanju, Ben and Dana and apprised them of the situation. He then sat back and pretended to doze, while watching the road coming up from the valley.

Three roads met at Raiagar—the road from Munsiyari, along which lay the village that Gautam called 'his village' and near which his estate was located, the road from Berinag, and the road from Almora-Barechhina. As roads were pushed through into interior Kumaon and tourist traffic burgeoned, junctions like Raiagar expanded rapidly and became serious commercial hubs-in-the-making. Grocery stores supplying nearby hotels and resorts, chai shops and dhabas serving tourist taxi drivers and their customers, and various small and mid-sized enterprises sprang up and a minor junction was well on the way to becoming a major market place.

Pandit's convoy roared into Raiagar in a small cloud of dust, scattering pedestrians and the odd foraging chicken, and stopped in front of the main 'general store'. Everyone save the French couple emerged, stretched and loitered by the vehicles, while Mintu and Alok went into the shop to buy provisions. Bhanu strolled over aimlessly, talking busily on his cellphone, saw the French couple in Mintu's vehicle, ignored a searching stare from Pandit and continued down the road.

'They have stopped to buy stuff from a grocery store. Dana, stop well outside the village and hold Ben there too. I'll let you know when they move.'

He then conveyed the current status to Gautam, stopped at a paan shop, bought a bottle of Coke and drank it slowly watching the Pandit team. His vehicle was parked on the road leading towards Gautam's place, a little beyond and not easily visible from the junction.

When the Pandit team moved out on the Berinag road, Bhanu advised everyone as he walked to his vehicle, started up and came back to the junction to wait for Dana and Ben.

'I'll go first, Dana, you next, and Ben brings up the rear. If they take off up some kuchha track, we're not to follow but just watch that point from a safe distance. The Colonel is afraid they might grab us or something!'

'I remember the tracks leading to the cabins we were held at,' said Dana. 'They are not too far off, so let's speed up or we won't know if they've gone up any of them and will have to go recee, which the Colonel doesn't want, right?'

'Right,' said Bhanu, gunned his SUV and started the chase.

38

Pandit, monitoring his back trail, could spot no motorbike following them. Instead, he saw a dusty SUV some distance away.

He shook his head impatiently and called Mintu. 'Once we get up the track, stop and we will switch vehicles. I'll drive up straight to the cabin and stash the Frenchies. You and your boys walk back and watch the road. If anyone is trailing us, grab them—alive, Mintu—and bring them up. Ashok will go up with me.'

'Sure boss. But I couldn't see anyone behind us from Raiagar,' replied Mintu.

'There is a dusty grey SUV, but it's too far away to know if it's the same as the one behind us from Kathgodam. We just have to see.'

'We should then slow down a little boss, let them catch up. If it's just some tourist taxi or whatever, it makes no difference—they will just go past—else they will see us going up the path and follow us and we'll take them.'

'Yes, good. Tell Ashok to slow down a little, not too much. Just so they can keep an eye on us and see us go up the track.'

Pandit's convoy slowed down gradually, but Bhanu was alert.

'They've slowed down just a little, boys and girls, so I'm slowing down too. Is this bait, perhaps?'

'God knows, Bhanu, but stay alert, you'll be coming to the turnoff to one of their hideouts,' said Dana. 'It's twenty minutes up the hill—narrow kuchha road and dense forest. The other cabin is another half-hour down the road and again fifteen minutes up the hill.'

'Ok. If they stop to check their back trail or whatever, I'll just drive on through and you all do the same. We'll turn around and come back from further down.'

'Right.'

Bhanu got lucky. The turns and twists of the mountain road enabled him to get a glimpse of Pandit's last vehicle turning up the kuchha road to the cottage from a long distance away.

'All right, folks,' he announced to his colleagues. 'They've gone up the first turnoff that Dana mentioned, but just to make sure they've not split up the party, I'll go on to the second turnoff to check. Dana follow me, Ben stay and watch this one from a safe distance.'

Half an hour later, Bhanu confirmed that no traffic had gone up to the second safe house and he and Dana returned, stopped at a suitable point short of the track and took up watching stations.

'We've got them bracketed, Colonel, but once it is dark we'll have to move in close,' he informed Gautam, who said he'd call back after finalizing his action plan.

39

'I think it's time for action,' said Gautam to Ruth and the Israelis, who had arrived, refreshed themselves and were sprawled, relaxed, in Gautam's house on various items of furniture. Like old soldiers everywhere, they too took their rest whenever they got the opportunity. 'It's getting cloudy very rapidly and it's close to sunset anyway. Assuming Pandit and team propose to hit us at night, they will be relaxing for a while now and will be off guard. We'll take about an hour and a half to get to Bhanu and gang, by which time it will be dark and probably raining. Good time for a quick and quiet strike.'

Ruth and the others considered the issue and agreed.

'Your friend, Sanju, will be upset at being cut out of the action,' remarked Ruth.

'Yes, but I don't want to wait and have to ambush them on public roads. Much better to do it in the forest. Easier for Sanju to clean up afterwards, too. Let me talk to him.'

Sanju protested at first but agreed to Gautam's logic. 'You have good backup now that the Tinauli folks have reached,' he conceded. 'Use Bhanu and Dana for the actual assault. I would rather not have civilians involved in gun battles, if possible.'

'I agree, but you talk to Ruth, because she refuses to

listen to me,' replied Gautam and handed Ruth the phone.

Sanju spoke to Ruth for several long minutes. By the end, Ruth looked resigned. Returning the phone to Gautam, she took a deep, rather angry breath. 'I'll come with you as backup and reserve on site along with my friends here,' she gestured at the three Israelis from Tinauli. 'You, Dana and Bhanu can be the assault team—it's a small cottage and you've studied the plan I drew for you—and any more people will be counterproductive. We'll cut off any escape attempts and generally hang around trying to be useful.'

'Thank you. We'll move in fifteen minutes and use both, your vehicle and mine. I'll inform Bhanu. I also want Dana to check if the track is being watched by Pandit's people.'

'You're putting my baby in the way of bullets and shit, Gautam! I'm devastated,' said Ruth in a little girl voice.

'Sorry, but there's no place in my Gypsy for all of us—I've got Sher Bahadur to put in some equipment and stuff in the back. Come on now, we'll talk later. Deborah, if you'll come with me, we have some planning to do; Ruth will take Yaakov and Reuben.'

40

'Ok guys, Colonel's orders are to scout the track and see if the enemy is on guard. Check and report is what he wants,' said Dana.

Thunder rumbled, lightening flashed and Dana paused, looked up and shook her head. The sky was overcast; thick black clouds blanketed the area horizon to horizon. Thunderstorms in the mountains can be violent and seriously terrifying—lightning strikes, landslides and flooded culverts are routine—and Dana had experience of these from earlier trips.

'It's going to be raining in minutes. Once it begins to pour, I'll move up the hill from here, I have some idea of how the track wanders up to the cottage. Bhanu will follow, keeping me in sight but just about, not too close. Once we hit the track, we will go down towards the road—that's where they should be, if they are there at all. Ben, you stay where you are watching the intersection. No communication except in emergency—the cellphone reception seems remarkable for this wilderness, so we can always text.'

The rain came down with a roar; Dana found a narrow cattle track and began moving up hill slowly, setting up a painstakingly slow cycle of reconnaissance—check, observe, move, stop, and repeat. Bhanu followed her closely.

~

Mintu had stationed himself and his two boys close to the main road in positions that enabled clear views of the take off point of the track to the cottage. He was on one side of the track, the other two on the other side. They had seen one SUV and one bike in quick succession drive down the road. Other than an overloaded sarkari bus there had been no traffic since.

When the rain started, Mintu summoned one of the boys. 'Go down to the road and walk down, say, two kilometres. If that bike and SUV were actually following us, they may have stopped and will be watching the access to our safe house. Go check, and if you spot them, come right back. Don't fuck around on your own, ok.'

Personally, Mintu thought Pandit was being a trifle paranoid; but Pandit had good instincts and Mintu was a good soldier.

~

Ben spotted Mintu's man when he came down the track, turned left and began walking down the road. He texted Dana and Bhanu, who stopped to consider the matter.

'As planned. Watch back,' texted Dana in reply and continued uphill.

When she reached the track, Dana signaled Bhanu to move parallel to her while she walked on the edge of the track, watchful and alert and ready to slip into the trees if necessary.

~

Mintu's scout, known as Pintu, spotted the SUV and the bike parked by the side of the road, stopped, watched for a long while, then called Mintu.

'One SUV and one bike here, boss. Nobody around here that I can see. If they go uphill a bit and have binocs, they can watch the track to the cabin.'

'Fuck,' replied Mintu. 'Just stay and watch for a while. See if you can spot them—and don't get spotted. Just watch and let me know if you spot anything in this fucking rain.'

'Sure, boss, but visibility is poor and growing worse.'

'I know. Watch as long as you can see something. Call me if you see them.'

Mintu called Pandit. 'We may have the fauji and his people in the area, boss. Not confirmed, but likely. The SUV and one bike are parked by the roadside a little way down the road.'

Pandit brooded for a while. 'If they are hostiles, they would want to bracket our track, right? The other bike would then be on the other side, stopped short. Now assume they are hostiles—what would they do? Three people would not try and storm our place, so they would keep close watch and wait for reinforcement, assuming they have reinforcement. Too many uncertainties here, Mintu, too many unknowns. What do you suggest?'

Mintu thought very fast. 'If they are the Colonel's people, then two will be the Israelis from Tinauli, where there are two more elderly ones, but soldiers, I'm told. So that makes four and the Colonel, five. The only unknowns are the two women Pradeep had grabbed. Let's assume they are also hostiles allied to the Colonel—how, we don't know. That makes a total team of seven. We are seven and we know they will be coming, so we prepare for them and wipe them out once and for all. The Colonel has no relatives, we know that, so we just grab the property, then work the system to adjust the paperwork. It'll take time and money, but we won't have the problem of this guy fingering us all the time. I think we should end it here, if we can.'

Pandit laughed harshly. 'Mintu Mobile—always clear and precise! Good thinking, but we need to hedge our bets a little. Get back to the cottage. We'll set up an outer perimeter closer to the cottage—don't have enough men. Get here quickly, we have work to do.'

Mintu summoned Pintu back and the three piled into their SUV parked on the track and drove up to the cottage.

Dana heard the vehicle start up, slipped into the trees and watched the threesome grind uphill carefully, given the rain and the narrow track.

'Three men in a Scorpio have just gone up to their safe house,' she reported to Gautam. 'Not sure if they've left anyone behind on guard duty.'

'Please check very carefully, Dana, they are slippery bastards, and get back to me. We are on our way and should be there in an hour.'

'Right, chief,' acknowledged Dana and continued down the track with Bhanu in parallel in the woods. Twenty minutes of careful scouting established that there were no hostiles on the track and Dana so informed Gautam.

'Right, now get Ben to you and the three of you remain concealed by the track close to the road. Be careful, Dana—I'll call when we are close.'

41

'I propose to take Dana and Bhanu and come up on this cottage from behind,' explained Gautam to Deborah. 'I've looked at detailed maps of the area and Joshiji has told me that a new road is being constructed that takes off from the Berinag road a little way after the tracks to Pandit's safe houses. He's not very clear about distances, but not too long a drive from Raiagar, he estimates. This road apparently curves around the hill and is to serve a group of villages that have been complaining for years of being cut-off from the main road. The kuchha road is ready, and presumably motorable, and will take us to the other side of the hill on which Pandit's cottage is located. We'll have to climb up and then come down behind the cottage. We'll just take a chance on the existence of pagdandis to do so.'

Deb nodded. 'These hills always have cattle tracks and footpaths—there are scattered villages all over.'

'Right. I want you to take charge of things on this side. Block the track—there's some equipment in the back that might help—and spread out short of the cottage and let no one get out. Spot their forward defense line, but take no action until we are in position. You have the walkie-talkies so we can communicate without relying on cellphones. Basically, I will ask you all to flush them out of the cottage, while we come from behind and take them out. Only one person, Ruth, is a sniper, so—only she is allowed to shoot towards the cottage, and that too if she has a clear view and shot at a hostile. I don't want any friendly fire on us. Simple, and I hope, effective. You can use Bhanu's SUV for blocking the passage.'

Deb smiled slightly. 'Simple is the only thing that works Colonel—as we both know. That and training and luck, of course.'

'Of course,' agreed Gautam and was quiet till they saw Ben's motorcycle parked by the road. A little way ahead, the track going uphill was visible and Gautam double dipped his headlights and stopped by the roadside.

Ruth's Jeep stopped behind Gautam's Gypsy and Dana and Bhanu came down to the road.

The war council was brief. An axe, a spade and a sabbal—a long heavy iron rod for shifting recalcitrant boulders and tree trunks—were unloaded along with a sack full of unspecified stuff, and Gautam, Dana and Bhanu drove away in search of the 'under construction' road.

~

Deb took command of the team smoothly and naturally.

'Ok, Ben and Yaakov, go up the hill, avoiding the track, and scout out the landscape. No action—just locate their forward posts and the best possible attack scenarios. I will give you a night vision device, the only one I have. The Colonel had two and I insisted he take one with him. So take care. Take two walkie-talkies—these were available in adequate numbers—but try not to talk, sound carries despite this rain. One of you come back here to report and one stay and watch. Go.'

Ruth fetched Bhanu's SUV and they used it to block the track. Then, in about half an hour, working in ten-minute shifts, they rolled a number of large stones and two biggish tree trunks they found lying on the hillside, across the relatively narrow track.

'That should stop any SUV quite effectively,' observed Deb, breathing a little hard after her last turn with the sabbal.

⁂

Ruth had briefed Yaakov about the track and cabin layout and he quickly briefed Ben and they moved off, Yaakov leading with the night vision device.

Forty-five minutes of a slow, slippery and stressful climb brought them within eyeshot of the last hairpin bend that led to the large, flat clearing where the cottage was located. They had spotted one advance guard, wet, miserable and restless, beneath a large oak tree just off the track. After a careful inch by inch scrutiny, they found one more professional goon in a reasonably concealed hide overlooking the track. Two substantial tree trunks blocked the track at the sharp bend, denying any motorized transport access to the cottage.

Yaakov signaled that he would stay on watch while Ben went back to brief Deb and party. The return was much faster despite the darkness—Ben was young, agile and blessed with excellent eyesight.

'I think we should all move up and when the Colonel is in position we take out the two outside and do something to flush the enemy out of the cottage. The Colonel then finishes the job. Only Ruth with the rifle and night-scope is allowed to shoot then. Clear?' observed Deb after Ben's briefing.

'How are we going to flush them out, Deb?' asked Ruth and Deborah smiled and hefted the sack that had accompanied Gautam and her from Gautam's place.

'Guess what's in here?' she said and without waiting for an answer gestured to Ben to lead the way up the hill.

Ben nodded and turned away back through the jungle towards the cottage.

42

A half-hour drive brought Gautam and team to a kuchha road taking off to the left. It wound around the back of the hill they had been driving along till then.

'Right, folks. This appears to be the road in question. Let's take a look,' said Gautam and in low gear took the steep gradient that faced him. The Gypsy had four-wheel drive and very soon it became evident that its services would be required shortly. The road was narrow, unmetalled and in very poor shape. The rain had converted the surface to slush and potholes; stones and mini boulders dotted the track.

'From the map I looked at, I estimate that we should go along for about five kilometres, stop and then start climbing. Of course, my estimate of the cottage's location is a little rough, but let's see.'

'You have the map here, Colonel?' asked Bhanu.

'Yes, on the back seat.'

'Oh wow! This is a detailed battle-worthy map, boss,' exclaimed Bhanu, picking up the heavy plastic sheathed document and peering at it by torchlight. He studied it for a long while and then put it down.

'You've got it right, more or less, Colonel, but we can stop about four kilometres down. I think it might be easier, though a little longer from there. I'll show you.'

'No need,' interrupted Gautam. 'Your map reading skills are probably in better shape than mine. You want to take a less steep route, right? And you are absolutely correct—that's what we will do. Provided we get there and not end up in the khudd.'

Gautam corrected a sudden skid and winced as something heavy crunched against the bottom of the vehicle.

'Come on, darling,' he muttered. 'Stay with me here—don't let me down now.'

The Gypsy responded valiantly to Gautam's request and the next few kilometres saw steady, if not spectacular, progress. Then their luck packed up. A substantial landslide blocked the road and a detailed inspection confirmed that there was no way the vehicle was going to get across without significant earthmoving work with serious equipment and a lot of labour, none of which was available.

'All right, people, we march from here on,' announced Gautam. 'Take a last look at the map, Bhanu, and lead us to the top of the mountain. We should be able to spot the cottage from there. They have a generator and use it, you said, Dana. We'll use our torches bindaas till we reach the top, and then be more careful—go with narrower beams from there. Let's go.'

Pandit had positioned Ashok and Billu as his first line of defence outside the cottage and retained Alok and Mintu and his team with him. He summoned Mintu with a nod and they stepped outside.

'I need a backup plan, Mintu, and it's a simple one. You take the Frenchies and Bhim Singh out of here now.

Bhim Singh has a hideout, some sort of cave, in the forest on the way to the other shack. Take them there, tie them up and leave Bhim in charge. Come back as quickly as you can. You will be the strategic reserve—outside the cottage with the one submachine gun I could manage from your friend in the ordinance depot. Anyway, eat first, then get going—we'll discuss things on your return. If they are indeed planning an assault, it won't be till late night.'

43

From the top of the ridge, Gautam and team surveyed the mountainside spread out below them. The rain had stopped, the clouds had dispersed as quickly as they had appeared and a near-full moon illuminated the landscape quite magically.

Pandit's retreat was clearly visible—the only bright, electrically lit up spot on the hillside.

'Ok, find a suitable passage down, Bhanu, and stay away from the burnt areas of the forest—we have time enough to go down slow and steady.'

'Right, boss,' replied Bhanu, checked out the slope carefully, and began to move down slowly.

Halfway to the target, Gautam called a halt and called Sanju on his cell.

'We've made good time, Buddha, and are an hour or so out,' Sanju told him. 'How are you doing?'

'Moving down to Pandit's shack from the ridge above. Should be in position in about half an hour, forty-five minutes.'

'Wait for us to reach, bro—if you can.'

'We'll scout the place and take a call, Sanju. Once in position, it's a pain hanging around in the damp jungle—not good tactics either. Anyway, I'll see.'

'Okey dokey,' said Sanju resignedly. 'You're the man on the spot, your decision is final.'

Stationed a safe distance away from the cottage's front door, Ben and Yaakov observed everything carefully, in great detail. The front line was being summoned one at a time, each going inside to fill themselves up with what Bhim Singh had to offer as sustenance.

Deb was informed of this new development and she reported it to Gautam.

'Good. Keep them spotted,' was Gautam's response as he followed Bhanu down the narrow cattle tracks meandering through the oak forest.

Meanwhile, Mintu had already left the cottage with the French couple and Bhim Singh, a good twenty minutes before Gautam and team halted at the edge of the forest. The cottage was located some way down the hill, beyond a few long-neglected terraces that indicated an attempt at cultivation some time ago. A rough footpath came by the side of the terraces and moved off along the hillside on the edge of the forest—the path Mintu had taken a while ago.

Bhanu grunted. 'Open space, Colonel, and the moon is providing reasonably clear visibility.'

'Let's scout a little. Go along the forest line, skirting the terraces on either side and see what the terrain is like. Dana, go right, Bhanu, left and check for approaches to the cottage that offer better cover than available here. Warn Deb—her people will be around the front of the cottage and we want no friendly fire nonsense. Be back in fifteen.'

Bhanu was back in ten minutes. 'No clear approach from the left, boss, too exposed.'

'Right. Let's see what Dana finds.'

Dana returned ten minutes later with better news and led them along the forest edge to a point from where they could skirt the terraces and approach the cottage from the side, under cover, till they hit the clearing in which the structure was located. The cottage was close to the edge of the clearing and the retaining wall of the terrace closest to it. A door opened out from the rear wall into the gap between the retaining wall and the cottage. Like all old hill structures, windows were small and resolutely shut against the weather; the only other access point appeared to be the front door.

Dana's description of the cottage layout had been clear. 'The front door opens into the living room beyond which is a corridor going down all the way to the back door. On the left, as you come from the living room, are two bedrooms one after another and on the right is a room—spare bedroom, perhaps—I don't know anything more as the door was closed—and following that is the kitchen. That's all we could gather in the time we were there.'

'Ok, let's get this done,' said Gautam as they stood just inside the tree line next to the clearing. 'Bhanu and I go along the retaining wall behind the cottage. I cover the back door, Bhanu, the far side, and Dana, this side. We wait for Deb to confirm that the two out front have been taken out. When Deb tosses a couple of Molotov cocktails—home-made, and I hope to God they work—to flush them out, we take them out. I may go in if I feel it necessary, nobody else. Careful who you shoot—don't kill the Frenchies.'

Gautam picked up his walkie-talkie, gave Deb the green light and the three moved carefully into position.

Deb signaled and as Ben and Yaakov moved forward to take out Pandit's advance guard, she readied the homemade petrol-bombs-in-wine-bottles and planned their disposition.

'You toss a couple onto that woodpile in the corner of the clearing beneath the tin sheet and hope it catches fire,' she instructed Reuben. 'I'll toss one at the front door and one through that front window. And our work is done.'

'You'll be exposed for a quite a while, Deb. Let me do the house and you do the wood stack,' protested Reuben.

Deb shook her head. 'We both have to step out into the open anyway, so both are exposed; and I have a better throwing arm. Just do as I say and get ready. The Colonel and the others should be in place soon.'

44

After the quick meal break, Ashok and Billu were back in position in the forest overlooking the track. Having eaten, they felt relaxed and a little sleepy—it had been a long day. The two younger Israelis reached their targets at about the same time, indicated their status and waited for Deb's signal.

'Go,' said Deb and she and Reuben stepped out into the clearing and flicked their lighters on.

Ashok and Billu saw two figures suddenly materialize out in the open. Clearly unprepared for this sudden assault, they frantically grabbed for their weapons, but crumpled to the ground instead as Ben and Yaakov opened fire.

With the front line successfully incapacitated, Reuben tossed one firebomb underhand at the woodpile, then followed it with the second and watched both explode into flames just where they were supposed to. The wood, protected from the rain by the tin sheet, caught fire almost immediately.

Deb's first cocktail hit the wooden front door bang-on, the glass broke and the petrol exploded with a gratifying whoosh. The second throw, however, missed its mark narrowly and hit the stone wall beside the window, splattering the wooden frame with burning gasoline, but not quite setting it alight. Shaking her head impatiently, Deb reached for the last bottle in the sack at her feet, lit the makeshift fuse and was poised to toss it at the window when the front door flew open and two men rushed out guns in hand.

Pandit had reacted very quickly when the two gunshots were heard and the front door caught fire. 'The front door—and don't shoot our people,' he yelled, picked up a heavy old armchair and smashed it into the burning door, which fell away, leaving the exit clear. Pintu and colleague moved immediately—they grabbed their weapons and rushed out of the gaping space where the door used to be, looking urgently for targets.

Deb saw the two men emerge from the house, swiveled a little and tossed the Molotov cocktail towards them. The bottle landed just ahead of the pair and exploded. Pintu, the more agile of the two, swerved away from the object flying towards them, dove to the ground and succeeded in getting away with second degree burns on his arm and side. His comrade, however, was not so lucky—a significant portion of the burning petrol splashed him liberally and he screamed in agony until a shot from Ruth's sniper rifle put an end to his misery.

Pandit, who was crouching just inside the doorframe, saw his henchmen go down and then spotted a figure holding a handgun backing away towards the trees. He aimed carefully, fired three times and saw the figure buckle and drop. A burst of fire from the edge of the forest made him roll aside and away from the open doorway.

Reuben saw Deb fall, fired a burst of shots at the dim crouching figure in the room beyond the doorway and ran to his partner. Ben too ran up, while Yaakov and Ruth maintained covering fire at the door. Yaakov stopped firing when they carried Deb into the woods, set her down and began checking for wounds, but kept a close watch for any movement.

'We're stopping firing, Colonel. Total four targets down—two frontline guards and two from the house. Deb hit—checking her.'

Gautam, having checked that the back door was bolted from the inside, waited outside till the firing stopped and Yaakov reported the action.

'Right, going in. Everyone maintain positions. Stop firing into the house,' he said on the walkie-talkie, and broke open the door with a powerful shoulder heave. As the door sagged open, Gautam tossed two flash bangs in quick succession into the corridor, followed them in and threw two more into the living room visible at the far end of the corridor.

The kitchen and the two bedrooms were clear, but it had cost him a few seconds to check them, so he tossed another f-n-b into the living room and darted in to see a disoriented Alok holding a gun and a flickering movement as a large body dove out of the open door space, rolled, got up and ran away. Gautam shot Alok four times, saw him fall, and stopped at the door when he heard a flurry of shots outside.

'Coming out of the front door—don't shoot me,' he

yelled into the communication device and ran out to find Bhanu down on the ground and Pandit—a big shadowy figure—scrambling up the terraces towards the woods. Gautam took careful aim and fired three times and thought he saw Pandit stumble, but the big man continued his uphill run and disappeared into the forest. Gautam grimaced and shoved his handgun into its holster—pistols are not the weapon of choice of armymen!

On examination, Bhanu was found to have taken three hits—two to the chest, which were stopped by the armoured vest he wore, but had none-the-less broken some ribs—and one to the upper arm, which had left a nasty wound that was bleeding profusely.

'Bhanu needs assistance,' he yelled out and when he saw Yaakov running towards them, patted Bhanu reassuringly and went in pursuit of Pandit.

45

Sanju had received the GPS coordinates of the cottage and the track leading to it and had been told that the track was blocked a little way off the main road.

'We are at your road block and walking up,' he told Deborah.

'Good. Take the path, but be careful, we are going into action very soon,' replied Deb.

Halfway up the track, the crackle of small arms fire filtered down through the forest and the distant glow of a large fire became visible.

By the time they reached the cottage, everything was quiet—Bhanu was being bandaged, Deb, who had also taken two bullets centre-mass but thanks to the vests provided by Gautam had suffered only one broken rib and a very painful bruise on the stomach, had already been bandaged; and Dana had followed Gautam into the woods in pursuit of Pandit, informing him on the walkie-talkie that she was doing so.

'If you permit, Sanjay, Farah and I will follow the Colonel. I presume the kidnapper is going to the kidnapped couple and we are here for them, after all,' said Didi. 'We'll be far enough behind them to not interfere in any…um… shooting match that may occur.'

Sanju looked speculatively at Didi and nodded after a moment's thought. 'Yaakov, please escort the ladies, will you. And ensure you have the full medical kit with you—when our friend Gautam is on the rampage, medical facilities become necessary. Take care, don't step on Buddha's heels—that's not good for health. Also tell Buddha and Dana you are following—she too reacts very quickly and violently.'

He then turned to the remaining team. 'Now that the wounded are strapped up, we will clear the roadblock and bring our vehicles up. We have a stretcher in one of them. Don't want the wounded to walk down to the road. We'll dispatch them in one vehicle to Almora. I've already spoken to our friend, Dr Pant, who luckily was holidaying at his Nainital house and is now on his way to Almora. I knew we would need his surgical skills. Dr Pant will attend to these people at his friend's new, well-equipped nursing home. Let's start cleaning up—transfer the bodies to the house and burn it comprehensively—nothing for an investigative reporter to find. Ok, let's go people.'

46

Pandit blundered into the woods, found the path that led to Bhim Singh's hideout and walked quickly along it. Bhanu had hit him once, but nothing seemed broken even though it hurt like hell. The 'bullet proof' vest he wore was of very good quality, a patently illegal acquisition facilitated by an avaricious stores' clerk in an elite state commando unit. Gautam had grazed him twice, but he ignored the hurt and kept moving.

'That bastard Colonel—has to be him!' Pandit muttered to himself. 'But I'll get him now! He doesn't know this path and I do. Come on, motherfucker, come to me and fucking die.'

Pandit shook himself and steadied down. He could see that the sudden and effective violence had shaken him. He had dished it out often enough, but never been on the receiving end. He started breathing deeply as he walked and planned how he would ambush those following him. Within a couple of minutes he blundered into Mintu returning from depositing the prisoners in Bhim Singh's cave.

'Fuck, I almost shot you there, Mintu,' said Pandit. 'Come on back to where you were—things have gone to shit back there. You lead. We'll talk as we walk—can't stop.'

Mintu, shocked to see the state Pandit was in,

immediately turned back and retraced his steps.

'What happened, boss? And what's the plan now?' he asked, urgently.

'They came early, torched the woodpile and the front door and crashed in from the back—several of them. Must have killed Ashok and his lad; your boys are gone too and I'm sure so is Alok. Just you and me here, now. I hit two of them, by the way—that reduces the odds a little.'

'But not much, boss. They still have five people as per our estimate—those are not good odds, boss. We should leave the Frenchies for them to find—that will slow them down a bit—and get away through the jungle. No point going up against five armed and trained soldiers. No point at all. We get down to the road, get a lift to Raiagar, take a taxi to Almora and reorganize things. They don't know about your Sattal place. We hole up there, call Dhami's two teams from Tehri, let everyone relax and then get back to them when they've forgotten about us.'

Pandit cracked a nasty smile. 'So, that's your considered advice, eh, wise old Mintu Mobile! We run, our tails between our legs, and live to fight another day! That's your fucking advice, the best you can do!' His voice rose almost to a shriek towards the end. 'I'm going to ambush those sons of bitches behind us and leave them dead in this stinking forest for the fucking wild boars to feast on. Remember that sharp dip this track takes a little way ahead and then rises steeply and turns and levels off? Remember the boulders by the side? We'll hunker down behind them, and as they reach the top of the incline a little slow and winded, we blast them to kingdom come and then take the Frenchies and walk down to the road. Any objections or suggestions, Mintu?'

Mintu shook his head. 'No, boss. That's a good place for an ambush. We can do it and get away if there aren't too many of them.'

'Now you're thinking, Mintu, instead of shitting yourself. Remember, I've hit two—they will need medical attention and transportation to the nearest hospital. They can't spare many hands to chase after us.'

Mintu nodded again and kept moving.

Gautam walked quickly but carefully along the path, alert for an ambush, and noticed a narrow but well-defined track taking off from the footpath he was on and heading up the hill in roughly the same direction. He stopped and waited for Dana to catch up.

'Let's take this pagdandi, just in case they are waiting for us somewhere along the track. It's going in the same direction and we can come down on them, if we spot them lying in ambush. Else we'll just take a little more time getting to them.'

Dana nodded and gestured for Gautam to lead. The path was quite steep but clearly visible in the moonlight filtering through the oak canopy. Their progress was slow but steady. At one point, it suddenly became very steep and Gautam had to get down on all fours and crawl up for almost thirty yards before it plunged down very sharply and then levelled out. As he negotiated the capricious track, Gautam caught a fleeting glimpse of what was evidently the path he had been following from the cottage, just a little way below the pagdandi he was on now. He was wondering whether to rejoin the earlier path or look for another route parallel and above it, when he glimpsed movement below him and heard faint sounds—wet leaves swishing, stones rattling. Gautam flattened himself on the ground and waved to Dana behind him, who followed suite. He leopard crawled very slowly down the path, stopping frequently to listen and look. A demanding ten minutes later, he found the track just below him and could see a burly figure crouched behind a big boulder facing the direction from which they had all been coming. This was Mintu Mobile. Pandit was not visible as he was well concealed, prone behind a huge old oak that had fallen over beside the track and offered an ideal ambush position. Gautam was, in any case, expecting just one person, not two.

As Gautam worked out a way of getting down to the track and getting a clear shot at the crouched figure below him, the Gods of War turned capricious. The ground on which Gautam was lying prone suddenly and without any warning gave way; Gautam slid downhill in a shower of wet mud, stones and oak leaves and landed on the path behind and facing away from Mintu Mobile.

Startled by the noise and the thump of something big landing on the path, Mintu swung round to find Gautam prone on the track behind him. He reacted very quickly, swiveling and bringing his handgun to bear on the recumbent figure. As Mintu was bringing his gun up, Gautam too moved, and very fast indeed. He drew his weapon from its holster on his right hip and twisted his upper body around to point his weapon at the substantial target that Mintu presented.

Mintu was first off the mark, and the bullet hit Gautam's right thigh, caused a nasty flesh wound—a deep gash—and embedded itself into the ground. As Mintu shifted his aim and triggered his second shot, which hit Gautam's left arm just below the shoulder blade, Gautam clamped down on the shock and pain and carefully fired three aimed shots, the first of which tore into Mintu's throat and the rest into his face. Mintu Mobile dropped dead instantly. But the danger was not yet averted. As Gautam looked down to see the extent of damage to his arm, Pandit loomed up behind the collapsed Mintu, weapon moving slowly and carefully towards Gautam's head.

'We're both dead!' was the thought that flashed across Gautam's mind as he shifted focus and aim to the new threat.

A volley of shots rang out and Pandit's head seemed to explode. While Gautam was confronting Mintu, Dana had slid down the short distance towards the lower path. From behind an ancient oak, she fired three carefully aimed shots at Pandit, who was bringing his weapon to bear on the prone Gautam, hitting her target every time.

She stepped down on the track, checked both Pandit and Mintu for signs of life and, not finding any, quickly went over to Gautam.

Both Dana and Gautam were carrying small emergency medical packs and Dana opened them and worked on stemming the bleeding from the leg wound.

'Will you call Sanju?' she said and Gautam complied and held the phone close to her face.

'I need medical assistance. The Colonel has been hit twice—upper arm and thigh. The bone in the arm is probably broken, but the bullet bounced out and it's bleeding badly; the thigh wound is a bleeder too, but it was an in and out. I'm trying to stop the bleeding and clean up the wounds.'

'Yaakov is close behind you and has a full battlefield med-kit—use it. I'll send a stretcher and people as soon as I get our vehicles up here. Patch him up, pump him full of antibiotics, painkillers and plasma, and keep him warm. He's tough, he'll survive,' replied Sanju.

Dana smiled at Gautam. 'Sanju is really worried, Colonel. You'd better get well and soon! My job is at stake!'

Having handed over the medical kit to Dana, who brushed away all offers of help, Yaakov and the French officials continued along the path, cautiously. Yaakov, who was scouting ahead, saw the fire first. They sneaked up very carefully and found Bhim Singh fast asleep on one side of the large fire, the young French couple on the other. After a careful scrutiny, they holstered their weapons and entered the cave.

'I'll check outside for any signs of hostiles,' whispered Farah and stepped back into the darkness.

'We'll wake them up and get them moving, right, Didi?' said Yaakov as he bent over the recumbent old man.

Suddenly, he heard the swish of a handgun emerging from a holster and turned quickly, anticipating danger. It was Didi, bringing her weapon up to bear on the groggy, young Frenchman lying beside the pretty, young white girl by the fire.

'Don't move, Yaakov. You can't draw faster than I can turn and shoot, and I don't want to do that. Just let me do my job here.'

She raised her gun to point at the center of the prone Frenchman's chest when a roar of gunfire erupted.

Two bullets blew Didi's head apart, splattering blood and brain matter all over Yaakov and everyone else in the confined space. The young couple woke up screaming and Bhim Singh jerked awake with a yell.

Farah, was standing at the entrance, hands raised, weapon pointing upwards.

'Don't shoot, Yaakov. I'm the good guy here. I'm putting my weapon away and will explain the circumstances.'

A little stunned, Yaakov, gun in one hand, wordlessly held out the other to take possession of Farah's weapon.

'You'd better explain to both Sanju and me together. Then we'll take a call,' he said before connecting with Sanju on the walkie-talkie.

47

Dr Vijay Pant—tall, bulky, and an old friend of Sanju's and Gautam's—emerged from the operating theatre and joined the group waiting in the small lounge of the newest nursing home in Almora. He took a cup of tea from the refreshments counter and sat down with a sigh next to Sanju.

'About time Gautam stopped all this gunslinging business. None of us is getting any younger. Anyway, he should be fine. It was a clean break of the humerus and I've nailed everything together and he should heal and recover full functionality. Lucky for him the nerves are intact. Once I discharge him—which won't be for a few days—I would like him to go to his place for recuperation rather than Delhi, Sanju. Clean air and all that stuff. It will also give me an excuse to spend some time at that lovely place and call it work!'

Dr Pant laughed gently and glanced at Ruth. 'Of course, he'll need a full-time nurse and a great deal of tender, loving care for a quick and complete recovery. The Matron here has a daughter who's just qualified from nursing school and is interning here. She would be ideal for the nursing part; Gautam should hire her for a month. The other patient—the lady—also needs recovery time and nursing care. She, I'm told, lives in some village in the wilderness. But that won't do for her—she should also stay at Gautam's for a while. Your young man was very lucky, Sanju—just two cracked ribs, nasty bruises and hurting muscles for a while—youth is wonderful! Now I'm going to grab some sleep and we'll get together for dinner at the hotel. The patients will be heavily sedated, so all of you should also get some rest. The staff here is very competent and will call me in case of any problems.'

With that the good doctor departed to the nearby hotel where all of them were staying, an old and gracious bungalow converted by a terai businessman into a charming little resort complete with a view of the snowy mountains in clear weather.

'It's morning and I can't sleep, not just yet, anyway. You guys get some rest and relieve me later,' said Ruth.

Sanju nodded agreement and led the team off for some well-deserved shut eye. It had been a hectic night, disposing off all evidence of the 'encounter' between an elite unit of a 'central police force' investigating a kidnapping and getting the wounded and two rather bewildered young French persons to Almora, where Dr Pant had been waiting.

A flurry of phone calls, from the mountains to Datta and from Datta to France had followed Farah's gunning down of Didi. The clarifications had, however, been quickly forthcoming.

'As you must have seen, Sanju, that young Frenchman in question is of mixed African-Arab descent. That he has degrees from the Sorbonne and a PhD from Yale is, of course, irrelevant to the father of the girl—a nasty old lily—white right-wing industrialist of the old aristocratic school. I'm not making up this dramatic bullshit, I swear. The Head of the French Service, even gave me details of the old fellow's ancestry, I kid you not! Anyway, apparently the father had been very unhappy about the liaison and the kidnapping was a great opportunity to do something about it. Our friend Didi was nearing retirement, had expensive tastes and an increasingly doubtful reputation—misuse of slush funds, excessive use of force—more killings than even the French Service found acceptable—and stuff like that. Apparently, the father got to Didi, gave her the assignment and pushed his golfing buddy, the President of the Republic, to send Didi along to ensure French oversight over the incompetent Indians. But you don't fuck with that old fox running the French Service, right? He, too, saw an opportunity and added Farah to the team with clear instructions to solve the Didi problem effectively and far from his backyard. And so ends the story. Send that young hit woman back right away—she goes straight to the airport and on to the first flight to Paris. I made it clear to that old bastard that I didn't appreciate his assassins running around over here. He laughed and said that if ever the need arose again, he will ask us to do the needful as we obviously had many qualified people for such jobs!'

Sanju laughed. 'She will be escorted to Delhi by one of my people. Have someone meet them at the airport with the ticket and put her on the plane. And what do I do with the kidnappees, for Heaven's sake? They plan to go to the US—they already have tickets.'

It was Datta's turn to laugh. 'Feed them, let them rest a day and again escort them to the airport. The guy's apparently got a teaching job in California and she's registered for a PhD there. Daddy didn't know this. The India trip was just a quick holiday before starting a new life far from Daddy dearest, at least that's what I have been told.'

'All right, Fatso, will do as you say. Bye for now.'

EPILOGUE

A month went by slowly and very peacefully at Gautam's Himalayan refuge. Deb and Reuben, after only a small protest, stayed in the newly built guest cottage. Datta and Annie visited for two weeks. It rained incessantly—as it often does in the mountains—and time was spent largely indoors, reading, arguing, and for those medically permitted, making substantial inroads into Gautam's alcohol stocks.

Annie talked a lot; Datta was quieter than usual.

'What's bothering you, O beloved?' Annie asked her spouse one night. 'Is it just the excessive booze and food or something more?'

Datta smiled at his wife. 'Can't hide anything from you can I, love? Not that I was trying to, but I don't like Gautam's depression one little bit. He hides it well, but the bugger is troubled and that's not good.'

'So speak to him, for Heaven's sake. You're friend and family combined—it's your job.'

Datta shook his head. 'When and if he wants to talk, he'll talk. Till then, we are just around and available. Now, I need to sleep—the last drink was one too many for my age.'

Dr Pant and his spouse visited at the end of the month to check up on the patients and pronounced them well on the road to recovery. Deb and Reuben left for Tinauli soon thereafter. Ruth had returned to work once Gautam was discharged from the hospital and had gone back to Delhi. The nurse was relieved with a substantial bonus and a glowing recommendation and Gautam settled down to a very quiet spell of rest and recuperation. Dr Pant had recommended a detailed exercise regimen that he followed religiously. The Internet, miraculously, continued to function though a trifle erratically, and Gautam was able to maintain regular communications with his friends, along with starting a new communications thread with the abbot at the Japanese monastery.

Six weeks after the encounter with Mintu and Pandit, Gautam drove down to Moradabad for a rigorous medical checkup.

'You've healed fine, but go easy for a while—don't put too much stress on the wounded limbs,' counselled Dr Pant sternly. 'Give the body—and the mind—time to get over the trauma before you start hurting it again.'

Gautam smiled, nodded and drove back home in a happy frame of mind. Dr Pant was obviously satisfied with the recovery and besides, Ruth was coming up for a few days.

Gautam and Ruth sat on a sofa in the verandah very early one morning, warmly wrapped in a shared blanket, sipping tea. The sky was heavily overcast and the occasional rumblings announced impending rain.

'I'm off to Japan for a month,' said Gautam, breaking a long and comfortable silence.

'When? And whatever for?' asked Ruth, surprised. 'You just came from there a short while ago?'

'Yes, I did, but I need to spend some time sorting things out and I feel I need the abbot's help. I asked him and after a bit of convincing, he agreed to let me return for a month.'

'But sort out what, my Colonel? Care to tell me?' said Ruth perturbed.

Gautam took a deep breath and a long sip. 'Look, I left the army because I feared I'd gotten too much into the shoot-'em-up mode. The stimulus of fear, anger, power and excitement was getting addictive. From being a good soldier, I was on my way to becoming a monster, who had started enjoying what he was doing—volunteering for any and every mad op. The system sees this and uses you mercilessly—I did more black ops than most people, because I was always willing, in fact, eager. Shifting to the mountains, I thought I'll work out whatever the compulsions driving this behaviour were and get over it, but this episode showed me it's still there. I need to do something about it. And the abbot can help. The only one who can, I feel. So, I have to go.'

Ruth shook her head doubtfully. 'This is some guru-pupil thingy, isn't it?'

'Well, yes. He's my teacher. He helps me dig into myself, see what there is and deal with it. It's difficult and takes time, but it has to be done.'

Ruth thought for a while, put down her mug of tea and smiled at Gautam. 'All right, my Colonel, sort yourself out, if you can, and come back to me healed and whole. I have a conference in London a month from now, so let's meet there and take a short holiday amongst the Brits and the beer. For now, I too have an announcement to make. The powers that be are shifting me back to Israel very soon. The order, I'm told, is already in process and will be issued shortly.'

'But you haven't finished your tenure here, have you?' said Gautam unable to hide his distress at this sudden blow.

'Rules are meant to be broken when the need arises, you know that very well, my Colonel,' replied Ruth. 'And no, don't say it! I am a soldier and war for us is always imminent. And desertion in times of war is treason, sir.'

Gautam shook his head but said nothing.

With a huge peal of thunder the skies opened up and it began to rain heavily. Ruth rested her head against Gautam's shoulder and for a very long time neither said a word, just looked out at the pouring rain.

'I want some more tea,' Gautam finally announced. 'How about you?'

Ruth shook herself out of her reverie, looked at Gautam and smiled brilliantly. 'Yes, I do, but afterwards, my Colonel.'

She stood up, took Gautam's hand and without another word led him into the house.

ACKNOWLEDGEMENTS

Without my wife Sandhya's encouragement, this book would not have been written.

Preeti Gill was instrumental in getting Ravi Singh to look at the manuscript and to publish it and its two predecessors as a three-volume series. She has always been the best of literary agents.

Ravi read and accepted the book and Dyuti assiduously edited it and made it fit for publication. Many thanks.